Life
Love
and
Laughter

6-16-99

Dear Ellie,

    As you embark on a new,
happy journey, may you truly
enjoy life, + love, + laughter,
experiencing all to their max.

    You are very special, and a
blessing to those whose lives your
touch.

    God bless you always!
    With love,
    Linda

Life Love and Laughter

The Spirituality of the Consciousness Examen

FATHER JIM VLAUN

Resurrection Press
Mineola • New York

First published in March 1999 by Resurrection Press, Ltd.
P.O. Box 248
Williston Park, NY 11596

ISBN 1-878718-43-6

Library of Congress Catalog Card Number 98-68010

Cover design by John Murello

Printed in the United States of America.

Dedication

For Mom and Dad

Thanks for a lifetime of funny and inspiring stories
lived with a plate of rigatoni and chicken!

An Offering of Self

Take, Lord, and receive all my liberty,
   my memory, my understanding,
   and my entire will,
   all that I have and call my own.
You have given it all to me.
To you, Lord, I return it.
Everything is yours; do with it as you will.
Give me only your love and your grace.
   That is enough for me.

— St. Ignatius

Table of Contents

Acknowledgements

THIS IS MY FIRST BOOK. I never dreamed that it would involve so many people and so much work! I am very grateful to the many people who have guided and challenged me through the process and helped me throughout my life to develop a friendship with Jesus.

I would like to thank the administration, faculty, staff, and families of St. John the Baptist High School for their inspirational work in the mission land; thanks to the priests, sisters, and holy people of Our Lady of Lourdes for caring for me, gratitude also to the people of St. Mary's and St. Anthony's for helping me to know Jesus in the breaking of the bread. I am grateful to my many friends in the Catholic Institute of the Food Industry whose generosity has helped me tremendously.

Thanks also to my many priest companions who have walked me through life thus far, especially my priest support group and friends: Jerry Cestare, Joseph DeGrocco, Michael Holzmann, Frank Nelson, Tom Saloy, and John White. Special gratitude to the religious women whose heroic lives of love have been an inspiration to me: Alfred Cashman O.S.F., Nancy Campkin C.S.J., Noreen Cleary S.C., Margaret Coppenrath S.C., Alice Patricia Dolan C.S.J., Terry Gallagher O.P., Marie Happ O.P., Noella Lachat O.S.F., Diane Liona C.S.J., Julia Murphy O.P., and Mary Alice Piil C.S.J.

Thanks are due to the families who have taught me an

important aspect of Jesus' presence: the Bouklas', the Briscoes, the Carusillo's, the Fierro's, the Kovalevich's, the Lace's, the Scorcia's, the Tortora's, Steve Scialdone, Nan Doherty and Barbara Walsh; you have taught me more than you could imagine about God's love.

There are some people who supported me in remarkable ways during the writing of this book. I thank Jennifer Gallagher for being the first to read the manuscript and encouraging me to continue; to my dear friend John Sureau for his many hours of advice and patience; to Emilie Cerar Mackney at Resurrection Press for her insightful editing and courage to take a chance on me; and to my secretary/surrogate mother/advisor/spiritual director/boss and friend, Sr. Rose Taranto O.P. for her typing and editing of the text again and again.

God is good to us and gives us wonderful people as examples and guardian angels. I have been lucky enough to be inspired by four wonderful and holy priests: Msgr. Peter A. Chiara, Msgr. Fred Schaefer, Msgr. Bill Jablonski and Msgr. Frank Gaeta. These men exemplify the teachings of Jesus in unique and exciting ways, and have helped me to develop my gifts—in addition to teaching me how to eat!

We are fortunate in our diocese to have Bishop John R. McGann as ordinary. He is a compassionate shepherd who has supported me throughout my priesthood and continues to do so in so many ways.

Last, I would like to thank the two people who have inspired me the most, my mother and father. They remain faithful to Jesus through personal tragedy and victory. Through witnessing both ecclesial sin and virtue, they have taught me what it is to be a disciple.

Foreword

Every scribe who has been instructed in the kingdom of heaven is like the head of a household who brings from his storeroom both the new and the old.

—MATTHEW 13:52

FR. JIM VLAUN HAS DONE THE AMAZING in his book, *Life, Love, and Laughter: The Spirituality of the Consciousness Examen.*

He has produced "The Old" from the storehouse of his life experience—his struggles, his love and his prayer—in the most beautiful packaging of "The New." The *Old* is a key ingredient of the *Examen of Consciousness* found in the Spiritual Exercises of St. Ignatius of Loyola. The *Examen* is a wonderful tool for prayerful reflection upon one's day. Fr. Jim, a masterful teacher, presents the teachings of St. Ignatius in the language, images and experiences of people living in today's world.

Few people have the gift of bringing the traditional up to date as does Fr. Jim. His ten years of priesthood have been a journey to a deeper understanding of the mystery of Jesus and of his participation in the priesthood of Jesus. In his book, Jim has written his personalized edition of *Confessions of St. Augustine.* His struggles, fears, feelings of inadequacy and inferiority, and even his sinfulness find a place on each page. But side by side with these elements is the gradual process of letting go and allowing Jesus to fill the chasms of his heart. It is a moving story to witness.

In many ways I see what has happened to Jim clearer than others. He spent his pastoral year at St. Anthony of Padua Church in Beautiful Rocky Point while I was the pastor there. Jim was a very happy, sincere, hard working and good seminarian. He loved life, people and food. (I'm not sure in what order!) When he was ordained he was what we would all describe as a good young priest with great promise.

Jim has fulfilled these expectations and then some. He is extremely successful. He is well known for his gifts with young people. His weekly radio program, *Religion and Rock*, is broadcast nationally. He is a highly regarded speaker, preacher, retreat master, writer, parish priest and high school chaplain.

But he has become something more. He has been touched by the Holy Spirit and has become a *real* priest —someone passionately in love with Jesus and His people. Jim has allowed the Lord to fill his struggles, failures, sins, pain and broken heart with His love and peace. The result is a man alive and in love with Love who shares that enthusiasm with everyone.

In presenting the Consciousness Examen, Jim is presenting a model of prayer that has worked for him all through his priesthood. In this book he guides us through the Ignatian steps of Prayer for Enlightenment, Reflective Thanksgiving, Survey of Actions, Contrition and Sorrow, and Resolution for the Future. The Examen connects each movement and action of the day with the presence of God. As we look back, we are looking ahead to the next opportunity to love and truly live.

Father Jim presents each of the steps of the Examen in the chapters of this book. Here is where you find his genius. Jim speaks our language. He appeals to us because he echoes our own experience. Jim amuses and touches us with story after story. We become experts on Nana's wooden spoon and Aunt Mary's broken figurine. We wait in line at the Motor Vehicle Bureau, Disney World and rejoice in the best pizzerias, mom's "thinking-of-you" cards, cannolis, bowls of rigatoni.

Jim's book is very unusual because there are so few theological, scriptural or liturgical books that speak to real people. So much of what is written just doesn't connect with the real life experience of people. Theology is beyond us in the wild blue yonder of the ivory tower; liturgy books read like restaurant reviews of classy restaurants rather than as the human exchange of love and fulfillment that are at the heart of the Eucharist. Scripture books often paint the picture of the aloof Lone Ranger Jesus, rather than the Passionate Lover Jesus reaching into our lives.

Jim teaches Ignatius powerfully. When we finish we are covered with spaghetti sauce and grated cheese; we've been to many dinners; we've met first-class characters, and we have laughed and celebrated the best kept secret of Catholicism—that Jesus Christ is the most alive, interesting, fascinating, captivating lover the world has ever known and you can never be satisfied until you possess Him completely in the kingdom. The other part of that secret is that His Church is the most wonderful and fascinating collection of characters who should be having the biggest party this side of the Pearly Gates. We truly are God's chosen people—not His frozen people. We're all sinners who have discovered we have a Savior who will never give up on us and will never leave us alone until we say "uncle" and allow Him to embrace us and love us.

Evangelization is one of the big buzz words of the New Millennium. Evangelization is nothing more and nothing less than advertising—with one big difference. We believe with all our heart and soul in the Product— Jesus—whom we are trying to sell. Not only do we believe in Him, we use Him, we live Him, we love Him and we share Him each day. The more we give Him away the more of Him we possess.

Jim Vlaun is a master at selling the Product. He is an irresistible salesman because his Product is his very life and heart. His book will make happy consumers of all of us.

Msgr. Francis X. Gaeta
St. Brigid Church
Westbury, New York

~ 1 ~

The Desert Experience

I CAN REMEMBER watching her stir the sauce. Nana didn't just stir it, she conducted it. There was more to this than just cooking some tomatoes on a Sunday; there was something special, something holy about what was going on. The way she held the wooden spoon, the way she tasted just the tip of the worn end of that spoon said something far more to me than: Nana is in the kitchen. It's true, the kitchen was her church; it was there that she taught about life. She told stories about our family, and masterfully cooked a wonderful meal at the same time. I was a roly-poly little five-year-old sitting at her side listening and perhaps more importantly, watching and occasionally tasting the sauce from the wooden spoon.

Some years after Nana died, I remember going to visit her sister, Aunt Mary. Aunt Mary conducted with her wooden spoon, too. She, too, knew how to talk and stir, taste and reveal, all the while being able to listen with more than just her ears. I was now a "college-seminarian" the Italian grand-nephew studying for the priesthood. I was the "golden child." Yet I hadn't made the connection between my Nana and my Aunt Mary at that time. I look back now and realize that both of them had made a remarkable connection: their God was present in the coming together of family to share a meal. They had albeit unknowingly, discovered the secret of the Incarnation: that God so loved the world that he sent his only Son, to live in it, eat in it, walk in it, "be" in it. They knew the Master. I knew theology.

It's one thing to know theology, and believe me, I think that is important. To know the Master takes much more work. It takes living. I couldn't make the connections. It was like the two men who recited the twenty-third psalm. The first was a famous actor who had memorized the verses and delivered them with beautiful Elizabethan splendor. The second was an elderly priest who recited the psalm from his old, worn breviary. At the end of the recitation, the actor said to the elderly priest, "I must bow to you father." The priest remarked that the actor had proclaimed the psalm with perfect enunciation and diction. The actor responded that he had merely memorized the words, and proclaimed them as he had learned them. "You," he said, "you Father, are far more eloquent than I; I know the words, but you know the Author."

Sometimes wisdom comes through the deserts of life. Like most of us, I was not enlightened until much later in my life. It takes life, lived intensely to know the Author of Life. To know healing, we must know brokenness; to know joy, we must know tears; to know love, we must know God.

Why start with a pot of sauce being stirred? I think it is the starting point because it was around the pot of sauce that I learned about life, and it is in celebrating the

Sunday meal with my family that I learned about God. It took me almost thirty years to figure this all out. Quite frankly, I don't propose to have it all figured out yet; but I have known *love*, and have experienced it most profoundly around the table. Interesting? Crazy? All the retreats, all the books, all the meditation, all the spiritual direction in my life doesn't come close to the profound Presence I have known around the table.

Now don't stop here! It doesn't end with a bowl of rigatoni! Eventually the experience leaks out and spills over into every aspect of life. Remarkably, one comes to realize that the incarnate God, our Lord Jesus, is quite present, extremely present, Really Present in the ordinariness of our lives. So, the table, small "t" has led me to The Table, big "T."

This book is the story of that journey—mine and yours. It is a journey of discovery that will help to uncover our God who is ever-present, ever-calling and ever-leading us to deeper union with himself. If you have ever doubted God, cursed God, laughed at God, or felt profound loneliness, keep reading. You are not alone. There is a way out of the desert, a way that leads to a wonderful oasis.

Indeed sometimes wisdom comes from the deserts of our lives. So let us begin where Jesus began, in the lonely, arid desert.

> At once the Spirit drove him out into the desert, and he remained in the desert for forty days, tempted by Satan. He was among wild beasts, and the angels ministered to him.
>
> MARK 1: 12-13

The Desert Experience

It was around the time of Aunt Mary; during my college-seminary days, that I decided to leave the seminary. I had been in the desert for almost a year. My prayer life was dead, or in a deep coma. I had good friends, great friends, but I was empty on the inside.

I remember well the Broadway show, "Pippin," which was about a young man's search for meaning and direction in life. Pippin tried everything, and found himself ultimately unsatisfied, he couldn't find what he called "his corner of the sky." It was only at the very end of the musical, when Pippin finds love, that he finds what he was meant to be: a lover.

Looking for your corner of the sky involves a common human dilemma: "the grass is always greener" syndrome. This syndrome strikes when we have to make a serious life choice; marriage, a job, a college, or any choice that affects life in general. What made it even more difficult for me was that things always looked better to me across the street. Growing up, the McCully family always had it better. The brothers and sisters all got along, their dad was a rather prominent doctor, and the kids were all great at sports. We were a struggling family that included a child with terminal illness, a son (me) who was not good or interested in sports, and a dad who commuted tirelessly into the city everyday to make a living. On our side of the street there were no country club memberships, no new cars, and seemingly little perfection. When I look back I see how blessed I was and how grateful I am for what I had, but when I was there, the grass was definitely greener at the McCully's house.

As a teenager, I thought the priesthood was a great idea. It seemed like a way to be a real do-gooder, a way to serve God and His people well. So I entered a college-seminary. Many of them were closing. The one I attended was a rather healthy place, with rather healthy young men. After settling in for a year or so, my eyes again drifted "across the street" and I liked what I saw on the other side. I had friends on the "outside" who prayed and yet lived a great life filled with fraternities and all night blasts. Here I was praying three times a day in a semi-monastic setting and feeling lifeless and deprived.

For me, prayer was one-sided and rather lonely. I didn't hear much at all from God. As a matter of fact, this God of mine was seemingly absent from my life. I was like Pippin; I couldn't figure out my corner of the sky. My problem was not the priests or the seminarians; my problem was me, and my relationship with God. I figured God must not want me in the seminary or I would have known by now. God would have made me happier and more fulfilled if God really wanted me as part of the "in" team.

So after months of "discernment" (the word still makes my skin crawl!), I made an appointment with my spiritual director to tell him the news: I was leaving. He took the news well. In fact, a bit too well for me. I expected a shocked look and begging voice, "Please, no, don't say that, the Church will die without you!" Instead, he sent me on my way and said to come back in the morning, and we would talk more.

The next morning I expected a big pep talk about the importance of priesthood, and how much I was needed.

Instead, the Spiritual Director of the seminary asked me to go to a monastery, and make a five-day silent retreat under the direction of the Trappist monks. He told me that I would be able to figure things out better there, and after the retreat, I could submit my final decision. I surprised myself and readily agreed to the retreat. I was hoping that maybe on retreat I would discover the right thing to do, and more importantly, maybe I would find this God who had seemingly left me in the desert for almost twelve months.

A Monastic Experience

I had stayed in monasteries before. All seminarians had to participate in retreats in a retreat house or a monastery, so I was relatively comfortable with a few days in the beautiful setting of a Trappist monastery.

To many, monastic life was an awesome experience; to me, it seemed easy. No offense intended, but it seemed a bit easy to live in the confines of a beautiful monastic setting on the side of a mountain, farming, cooking, doing whatever, somewhat stress-free. Face it: no worries about taxes, no kids or loud music, no commuting, no major distractions. To me monastic life was a bit easier than being "of the world." Nonetheless, monks were holy people, dedicated to Jesus, and dedicated to serving him in a very particular way.

I settled into my cell around 4:00 p.m., with very little fanfare. Monasteries are places of silence and reflection and this one was pretty typical in that regard. The monks live their lives in accord with nature, so as the sun was setting, it was the natural end of the day for the community. I participated in evening prayer, ate a quick vegetarian dinner, and decided to go to bed.

The next morning, I was up at 5:00 a.m., sleepily praying morning prayer with the community in the guest gallery. Immediately afterwards, I proceeded silently with the monks to their refectory.

An interesting thing about many monks I have met is that they like to eat. They also like to cook. Being a kindred spirit on both of these charisms, I was looking forward to a wonderful breakfast. The smell of baking bread was distracting me in the chapel during morning prayer, and the thought of breakfast moved me quickly to the refectory. Most of the monks had gotten there before me, and they were sitting singly all over the refectory. As I looked around, I could see the vast vegetarian breakfast laid out on a huge wooden buffet table at one end of the room. The monks sat on wooden chairs at wooden tables picking away silently at muffins, fruit and some cheese.

God knows I wanted to eat, but I was taught by my parents not to make a pig of myself in public (is it acceptable in private?). To make them proud, I took a tray, placed an orange, a cup of coffee, and a small cranberry muffin on it, and took my place amid the silence. I was peeling my orange when I heard what seemed like a bull enter our little monastic china shop. It was a very large monk, scruffy, seemingly unshaven for months, who entered the refectory and made his way toward the table full of breakfast treats. I had a perfect vantage point to observe him from my seat. He took a tray, and began to shovel fruit, muffins, bread, cheese, hot cereal, and coffee on it. I knew that I liked this man very much! He looked around with that full tray and literally caught me staring at him. This led him immediately to my table where he plopped down his tray and began to eat.

Within a minute or so he said, "What's your name kid?" I told him, and he asked me why I was visiting the monastery, since I was clearly too young to be making an ordination retreat, and I didn't look like monk material with my baseball jersey and jeans. I told him briefly that I was thinking of leaving the seminary, and was advised to come to the monastery to pray and to reflect about my decision.

"What is it, a woman or something?" he asked. I told him that it was not a woman, and certainly not a "something"! I explained that it had to do with the fact that my prayer life was dried up, and at 20, I felt that God had sort of abandoned me. He hardly raised an eyebrow at this revelation, in fact, he kind of laughed. All the while he shoveled, eating like he had a date with the electric chair. I knew I liked him. Suddenly he stopped eating, stared at me a moment, wiped some crumbs from his scruffy beard and said "Kid, I can help you."

On the table was a pink index card. It had been folded in half to make a little table sign. On it was written, "Milk is in the refrigerator." My friend took this card and ripped it in half, and then reaching into his massive monk's habit, he pulled out a pen and scribbled five phrases on the ripped card. He looked up and handed me the card saying, "Kid, do this every day and you'll never feel that way again; these five things will save your spiritual life."

I stuck the card in my pocket and we finished our breakfast in silence. I remember marveling at his rotund figure leaving the refectory, not unlike a swarm of locusts leaving a cornfield having done their deed. I remember reading the pink card once at the table and not understanding it at first. But as days wore on, those five statements took on meaning. The card had these five simple phrases written on it:

> *prayer for enlightenment*
> *reflective thanksgiving*
> *survey of actions*
> *contrition and sorrow*
> *resolution for the future*

Although I never saw the monk again, I read that pink index card over hundreds of times, and as I started to do what the card said, the results were miraculous. Within days I felt my God in a way I never experienced God before. I knew then what everyone meant when they talked about what it was to be born again.

I went back to the seminary renewed. I taped that ripped index card on my bathroom mirror, and I did what it told me every day thereafter. This was not a phase or a spiritual moment; it was a turning point, and I have read that card every day for the past fifteen years. I look at that card which has moved with me from bathroom to bathroom, and I continue to do these five things. It was the way God reached me, and it has been my way to him through prayer and ministry. It helped me to find "my corner of the sky."

The Five Steps

I want to share this card with you. Why does it take a book to do so? Because it takes a great deal of reflection and life fully-lived to discover just how important this little five-step process is. I found out much later from my spiritual director that my monk friend didn't make this five-step process up—Saint Ignatius did. It is called the "Consciousness Examen," and for me it has been the road to Jesus.

The secret of the card is that it is the map to a process that allows one to discover the powerful presence of God in every single moment of our lives. Each one of the phrases is a life journey in itself. Combined, they become a lifestyle that can change one's thinking and help shed the trappings of our traditional view of Jesus and God the creator. It could be the key to knowing God as intimately as my Nana and Aunt Mary did. I'd bet a big bowl of rigatoni on that any day!

Consciousness Examen

1. A Prayer for Enlightenment

2. Reflective Thanksgiving

3. Survey of Actions

4. Contrition and Sorrow

5. Resolution for Future

Milk is in the fridge!

~ 2 ~

The Consciousness Examen

The Family Connection

IT'S HARD TO BELIEVE that a saint from the 16th Century could develop something so ideal for a people on the verge of the 21st century. I do believe that there are common threads in creation, and certainly, the most prominent is the presence of God in it all. After reflecting about this for a long time, I think this is why the Consciousness Examen is so timeless.

The Spiritual Exercises of St. Ignatius of Loyola was first published in 1548. I got my first copy of it in 1984. I found it in a garbage pail. Someone in my dormitory hallway who was not going on to study for the priesthood was dumping everything. This was a rather common practice throughout my years in the seminary. We would often gather like buzzards to pick through the "dead carcass" looking for valuable meat.

So I picked the copy of *The Spiritual Exercises of St. Ignatius of Loyola* out of the garbage pail, and figured it might come in handy. I didn't know yet that my new form of meditation and prayer, not to mention my new lease on my spiritual life was contained in its pages. I made this discovery while leafing through my garbage-pail book. The sections are well numbered in the Spiritual Exercises, and it is in the section numbered forty-three that the Consciousness Examen was named, and explained:

"The first point is to give thanks to God our Lord for the benefits received.

The second, to ask for the grace to know our sins and cast them out.

The third, to ask account of our soul from the hour that we rose up to the present Examen, hour by hour, or period by period: and first as to thoughts, and then as to words, and then as to acts . . .

The fourth, to ask pardon of God our Lord for the faults.

The fifth, to purpose amendment with His grace."

One can imagine my astonishment at finding these words in a book from the garbage pail! Why a Trappist monk, following the rule of St. Benedict, would quote the rule of St. Ignatius, the founder of the Jesuits, to a diocesan kid, who later picked the book out of the garbage is quite amazing to me!

Family Roots

But actually, it makes sense. Ultimately, the Consciousness Examen is rooted in the Gospel, and perhaps more profoundly in the Incarnation. Take a look at the genealogy from St. Matthew:

> An account of the genealogy of Jesus the Messiah, the son of David, the son of Abraham.
>
> Abraham was the father of Isaac, and Isaac the father of Jacob, and Jacob the father of Judah and his brothers,

and Judah the father of Perez and Zerah by Tamar, and Perez the father of Hezron, and Hezron the father of Aram,

and Aram the father of Aminadab, and Aminadab the father of Nahshon, and Nahshon the father of Salmon,

and Salmon the father of Boaz by Rahab, and Boaz the father of Obed by Ruth and Obed the father of Jesse,

and Jesse the father of King David.

And David was the father of Solomon by the wife of Uriah,

and Solomon the father of Rehoboam, and Rehoboam the father of Abijah, and Abijah the father of Asaph,

and Asaph the father of Jehoshaphat, and Jehoshaphat the father of Joram, and Joram the father of Uzziah,

and Uzziah the father of Jotham, and Jotham the father of Ahaz, and Ahaz the father of Hezekiah,

and Hezekiah the father of Manasseh, and Manasseh the father of Amos, and Amos the father of Josiah,

and Josiah the father of Jechoniah and his brothers, at the time of the deportation to Babylon.

And after the deportation to Babylon: Jechoniah was the father of Salathiel, and Salathiel the father of Zerubbabel,

and Zerubbabel the father of Abiud, and Abiud the father of Eliakim, and Eliakim the father of Azor,

and Azor the father of Zadok, and Zadok the father of Achim, and Achim the father of Eliud,

and Eliud the father of Eleazar, and Eleazar the father of Matthan, and Matthan the father of Jacob,

and Jacob the father of Joseph the husband of Mary, of whom Jesus was born, who is called the Messiah.

MATTHEW 1:1-16 (NRSV)

I love to read this Gospel on Christmas Eve. People fidget, eyes roll, kids cry, and yet it is important to have the names proclaimed. This is Jesus' family tree—the most important family that ever lived.

Impressive crowd huh? Take a walk down memory lane and explore some of the names on this genealogy for a moment. For example, Rahab was a harlot of Jericho:

> Then Joshua, son of Nun, secretly sent out two spies from Shittim, saying, "Go, reconnoiter the land and Jericho." When the two reached Jericho, they went into the house of a harlot named Rahab, where they lodged.
>
> But a report was brought to the king of Jericho that some Israelites had come there that night to spy out the land.
>
> So the king of Jericho sent Rahab the order, "Put out the visitors who have entered your house, for they have come to spy out the entire land."
>
> The woman had taken the two men and hidden them, so she said, "True, the men you speak of came to me, but I did not know where they came from.
>
> At dark, when it was time for the gate to be shut, they left, and I do not know where they went. You will have to pursue them immediately to overtake them."
>
> Now, she had led them to the roof, and hidden them among her stalks of flax spread out there.
>
> But the pursuers set out along the way to the fords of the Jordan, and once they had left, the gate was shut.
>
> JOSHUA 2:1-7

Then there is Ruth, she was a Moabite, and they get theirs in Deuteronomy:

No Moabite shall enter the assembly of the Lord; even to the tenth generation none belonging to them shall enter the assembly of the Lord forever. Ruth was part of an alien and hated people! Tamar was a deliberate seducer and an adulteress.

BASED ON DEUTERONOMY 23:4

Bathsheba, the mother of Solomon, was the woman David seduced from Uriah, her husband, with an unforgivable cruelty (2 Sam 11):

At the turn of the year, when kings go out on campaign, David sent out Joab along with his officers and the army of Israel, and they ravaged the Ammonites and besieged Rabbah. David, however, remained in Jerusalem.

One evening David rose from his siesta and strolled about on the roof of the palace. From the roof he saw a woman bathing, who was very beautiful.

David had inquiries made about the woman and was told, "She is Bathsheba, daughter of Eliam, and wife of [Joab's armor-bearer] Uriah the Hittite."

Then David sent messengers and took her. When she came to him, he had relations with her, at a time when she was just purified after her monthly period. She then returned to her house.

But the woman had conceived, and sent the information to David, "I am with child."

David therefore sent a message to Joab, "Send me Uriah the Hittite." So Joab sent Uriah to David.

When he came, David questioned him about Joab, the soldiers, and how the war was going, and Uriah answered that all was well.

David then said to Uriah, "Go down to your house and bathe your feet." Uriah left the palace, and a portion was sent out after him from the king's table.

But Uriah slept at the entrance of the royal palace with the other officers of his lord, and did not go down to his own house.

David was told that Uriah had not gone home. So he said to Uriah, "Have you not come from a journey? Why, then, did you not go down to your house?"

Uriah answered David, "The ark and Israel and Judah are lodged in tents, and my lord Joab and your majesty's servants are encamped in the open field. Can I go home to eat and to drink and to sleep with my wife? As the LORD lives and as you live, I will do no such thing."

Then David said to Uriah, "Stay here today also, I shall dismiss you tomorrow." So Uriah remained in Jerusalem that day. On the day following,

David summoned him, and he ate and drank with David, who made him drunk. But in the evening he went out to sleep on his bed among his lord's servants, and did not go down to his home.

The next morning David wrote a letter to Joab which he sent by Uriah.

In it he directed: "Place Uriah up front, where the fighting is fierce. Then pull back and leave him to be struck down dead."

So while Joab was besieging the city, he assigned Uriah to a place where he knew the defenders were strong.

When the men of the city made a sortie against Joab, some officers of David's army fell, and among them Uriah the Hittite died.

Then Joab sent David a report of all the details of the battle, instructing the messenger, "When you have finished giving the king all the details of the battle,

the king may become angry and say to you: 'Why did you go near the city to fight? Did you not know that they would shoot from the wall above?

Who killed Abimelech, son of Jerubbaal? Was it not a woman who threw a millstone down on him from the wall above, so that he died in Thebez? Why did you go near the wall?' Then you in turn shall say, 'Your servant Uriah the Hittite is also dead.'"

The messenger set out, and on his arrival he relayed to David all the details as Joab had instructed him.

He told David: "The men had us at a disadvantage and came out into the open against us, but we pushed them back to the entrance of the city gate.

Then the archers shot at your servants from the wall above, and some of the king's servants died, among them your servant Uriah."

David said to the messenger: "This is what you shall convey to Joab: 'Do not be chagrined at this, for the sword devours now here and now there. Strengthen your attack on the city and destroy it.' Encourage him."

When the wife of Uriah heard that her husband had died, she mourned her lord.

But once the mourning was over, David sent for her and brought her into his house. She became his wife and bore him a son. But the LORD was displeased with what David had done.

2 SAMUEL 11:1-27

And, these are just *four* of the characters on the family tree of Jesus. This crowd is more colorful than any soap opera, let alone our own families. In his infinite wisdom, it seems evident to scripture scholars that Matthew left out a few unmentionables along the way.

Matthew's genealogy is a gathering of very human people, adulterers, liars, cheats, mobsters, and holy people all mixed together. There is something wonderful about this! If any of us took a look back into our family tree, would we not find a similar list? If our God can send his only Son into this world through a very human lineage, what does that say of ours? I believe it makes ours holy, too.

The Consciousness Examen As A Means of Identity

A holy lineage; think of it! Our family has a holy lineage. Not only do our families participate in the lineage of the Incarnation, we as individuals do the same. At the heart of the Consciousness Examen is the simple fact that if God can choose to physically enter the world in time and space through a sinful human family, our time, our space and yes, our family can be a similar vehicle.

Easier said than done, you say. You haven't seen my family and my friends! Sure it's hard to believe. Is it possible that God could be as intensely present in our life as God is present in the life of St. Teresa of Avila or Dorothy Day or St. Francis of Assisi? It's hard to swallow.

I think the bottom line is that the intense presence of God is not something up to God; in many ways it is up to us. God doesn't decide to give one person more or less of God; each of us gets the whole deal. Allowing God to work in and through us is our responsibility.

Let's take the pope. He is certainly considered to be a

man who is in tune with the presence of God in his life. When you are near him, you immediately know you are around someone special. Not long ago, I was invited to celebrate Mass with him in his apartment. It was a very moving experience for me, not because of his holiness or notoriety, but because of the ordinariness of the man. I remember vividly being led through the long corridors of the Vatican to the papal apartments, and finally to a small chapel outside his bedroom. Walking into the chapel my eyes immediately focused on the back of the man sitting before the altar who many call the most powerful man in the world.

After a very simple Mass, we moved to his living room. The pope came forward and greeted each of us privately. What do you say to a pope? "Nice day!" "How about those Mets?" I could tell as he approached me that he was looking at my rather full Italian figure, and with a smile on his face he grabbed my cheek and said, "What a nice round face you have!"

My only response was to be completely human with this man. Very naturally I asked , "Holy Father, where is the best pizza in Rome?" Without even a breath, he looked right into my eyes with his deep blue eyes and said, "It looks like you have already found the best pizza in Rome!"

What a wonderful moment! A very human man sharing his humanity with me. I left the Vatican that day more deeply connected to God because I was more deeply connected to another person—in this case the leader of Christianity on earth. I had met a man of inner holiness; a man who knew the Author, not just the psalm.

The humanity crisis is really at the heart of what experts are calling the "Vocation Crisis." Seminaries today are not even near capacity. It could be connected with a humanity crisis. Allow me to explain.

I am often asked—even by my parents—why I remain a priest. I don't stay because of any great virtue; I wish I could claim that. It is simply who I have become. By the grace of God, this is me. Like a baker who bakes, a writer who writes, a mother who mothers, a father who fathers, I am a priest. The great Consciousness Examen teaches this. Whoever God has called you to be, fully become that. Pray every day to become more fully who you have been called to be.

I remember every year at the seminary around ordination time, a disease would strike the seminarians. It was ordination illness. Guys would become obsessed with vesture, black suits, leather breviaries, chalices, and everything else connected with ordination. Most of us got over ordination illness, but some had the disease in a chronic state. Some of them ended up unhappy priests, actually, miserable priests because their identity was found in the externals. Priesthood wasn't who they were, it was what they did. No humanity.

The Consciousness Examen teaches identity through humanity. Namely, that who we are is caught up in the presence of a God who is pure Love. We are called to be lovers. That is the starting point. Each person is an irreplaceable part of God's plan. Remember the old slogan on buttons and bumperstickers: "God doesn't make junk." It still holds true! Jesus tells us, "Love your neighbor as yourself." There's a big presupposition here, namely that we love ourselves. We just can't love others unless we love ourselves.

Even when we learn this concept as children, we somehow lose it in our teenage years. I work at a high school in the midst of one thousand teenagers everyday. The saddest part of my work is the fact that the young people I see each day don't recognize their talent, their beauty, their greatness in God's eyes. Young people today basically hate themselves and they are under enormous pressure. Drugs, violence, and sex pale next to the lack of love they feel for themselves and from their family and friends.

People ask me what I do at school. My job is so easy—yet so impossible—I am embarrassed to tell them. I basically help our kids to see that they are good and lovable. Teenagers need to know they are loved. So do the rest of us. To know you are loved and are lovable is to exist knowing the presence of God. We don't have to be self-righteous and obnoxious about our gifts. Nobody likes that. But to know that with all our brokenness and shortcomings, we are lovable, there's the ticket!

I think the pope knows that and that's what makes him such a great example to me. Since he knows God's love for him intensely, he can easily love others. It's impossible to hate yourself and love others well. Something suffers in our ability to love when we dislike ourselves.

Certain people have a special talent for making us feel good. Fred Rogers is one of them. Remember *Mister Rogers Neighborhood*? The whole premise of Fred Rogers' ministry is that you are special; there is nobody in the whole wide world quite like you. I met Fred Rogers some years ago at a youth conference where I gave a workshop. He was the main speaker, and I was able to sit next to him in the speaker's lounge and have a sandwich. I expected that in real life he wouldn't be as warm as his TV persona. Tread lightly, I thought. In reality, he was a wonderful, kind man, just like Mr. Rogers on television, and being with him made me feel good about myself. He is a master of making others feel good. Here is something Mr. Rogers wrote about love in his book, *How Families Grow:*

"Love, whatever it is, is essential for a human being's healthy emotional growth. That nourishment has many ingredients. We couldn't list them any more than we could list all the foods that give our bodies nourishment, but here are a few things that might appear on a list [about love].

There's liking, feeling affectionate toward, needing to be dependent on, needing to be in control of. We'd want to put friendship and companionship on the list as well as attachment, physical attraction, passion and sexuality . . .I find it helpful to think about love as separate from any of its possible ingredients. It's a different kind of thing. Love is like "infinity"; you can't have more or less infinity and you can't compare two things if they are equally infinite. Infinity just is and that's the way I think love is too. That may be the most one can hope to say, but when love is there. . .well, that's saying more than enough!"

Amazing! When you know love, you touch the infinite. Way to go Fred! Even in the great climax of *Les Miserables* the words ring out in my mind: "To love another person is to see the face of God."

Fred Rogers and Victor Hugo may not have known it, but they were doing the Consciousness Examen. When you know love that powerful, you know God. That kind of love doesn't happen only in a monastery, it happens in our homes, too.

Even Ignatius of Loyola knew this. That is why he made provision in his Consciousness Examen for a "portable" version of monastic living. Not everyone is called to monastic life, but we are all called to holiness. St. Ignatius provides a way for most of us with his "Nineteenth Annotation."

The Way to Love:
The Consciousness Examen As a Form of Prayer

In the Spiritual Exercises St. Ignatius provides the "Nineteenth Annotation," that acknowledges the life of a person of "education or ability" who desires a spiritual life, but cannot enter a monastery or convent. He explains that the Consciousness Examen can be done each day and will lead to a state of holiness that is comparable to monastic living. In order to be successful at this spiritual "exercise" one must also embrace a "missionary spirit."

This year our school began with a day of prayer for our faculty and administration given by a wonderful priest, Fr. Peter Chiara, who dedicated the day to "The educator as missionary." Father Peter stressed the need for a missionary zeal in order to work successfully and wholeheartedly with teenagers.

The day ended with a Mass. During the Mass, some of us posted a simple sign on every faculty room door throughout the building. It read: "You are now entering the mission land." Something remarkable happened that day. Our faculty began to recognize the missionary zeal inside of themselves. Teaching in a Catholic school has to be more than a career; it must be a missionary vocation to carry the good news to new ears and eyes.

A school is not our only mission land. Every time we leave our home, drive our car, shop for food, hold a hand, share a thought, offer a smile or lend a hand we enter the missionary land of Jesus. But for most of us, the mission land is a place that is far away. We send money to *them*. *They* live in hot, undeveloped places that need to hear the message of Jesus. How did we ever get this impression? It is probably because of the good and holy missionary priests who serve the poor in third world countries. Although this is noble work, we don't want to miss the mission land in which we live and work and the poverty that exists all around us.

Historically, the people that led holy and prophetic lives outside of the monasteries were the missionaries. Look at the saints. There are literally hundreds of saints that are "externs," living a life of radical Christian living outside of the monastery. Many of our "favorite saints" are "externs": Francis, Dominic, Clare, Teresa, and Mother Cabrini to name a few.

It seems that as we turn the page on the millennium, we too are called to a similar life, namely radical Christian living. That's what St. Ignatius' Nineteenth Annotation is all about. A call from our Lord to live the gospel *in* the world, not away from the world. This has a rather solid foundation in the gospel of John where Jesus prays for his disciples who are called to be *of* the world, not *out* of the world.

We sometimes forget that the disciples were of the world—plaster or pictures make them seem "other worldly." That's why I love the Acts of the Apostles. The humanity of the disciples is very evident. It is really like a soap opera of the early church! It tells the story of the early disciples of Jesus struggling with being "of the world." At one point, "the community of believers were of one mind and heart, sharing everything with one another and living in common." Then three chapters later they are splitting up, arguing, fighting, and ready to throw in the towel! You know when I first learned about all this in the seminary, I was scandalized. I couldn't believe that there was so much dissension in the early church. Now, it is my greatest source of strength!

Church is messy. Discipleship is messy. That's why the Nineteenth Annotation is such a wonderful source of strength for us. It is our way to see Jesus through the messiness. The secret is this: the only way through the mess is to embrace the presence of God in all that we are and all that we do; even the most unlikely things of the world.

Let's take rock music and rock stars. I am lucky enough to host a nationally syndicated radio program called, "Religion and Rock." The show has been on the radio for almost twenty-five years now, and I have been the host for the last nine. Our format is simple: play ten rock songs that have a similar theme, like forgiveness, friendship, etc. In between the songs, I do a little "sermonette." Every five weeks or so we invite a band or artist as a special guest to talk about their music and how God has played a part in it. I have been shocked time and time again to hear people like Paul McCartney, Elton John, and Hootie and the Blowfish explain how God uses their music to convey a message. These people know that God is using them, and on some level, conscious or not, they have experienced the missionary call of Jesus. They struggle to live that message and share it with others.

What a great example to us! Not only are rock stars living lives of Christian values, but they have responded to God's call to "co-creatorship" in order to help make the message known. That is what the Nineteenth Annotation is all about. We are part of the story. It doesn't end with the last chapter of the Acts of the Apostles; the story continues to be written through and in us. Our goal as a people struggling to make sense of our lives, is to continue to write the Acts of the Apostles and to call others into the story by our example.

And what a wonderful story it is. There really is good news here! Think about it. Every move we make, everything we do, is graced by the presence of a loving God who accepts us as we are. It wasn't that easy for Jesus who had to deal constantly with the Pharisees non-acceptance. In fact they looked for every opportunity to catch him off guard. Imagine living like that. I call it "sweatshop spirituality." Sweatshop spirituality takes place in an environment (on the job or at home) where one is given orders, intimidated, and always nervous about the "rules." Sweatshop workers fear losing their job, making the quota, and of course, angering the boss.

Lay and ordained ministers in our church can get caught up in the "sweatshop" mode—worrying incessantly about following every rule, making sure every liturgical law is followed perfectly, and trying to keep on the "right path." Leave me out of this church please! This church is the church of the Pharisees, a joyless church where everyone lives in fear. Jesus called the Pharisees out of fear and into life. Some bought it; some did not. Two thousand years later, we're still seeing sweatshop Catholics from the top down who bully others around. It makes me sad to see people imprisoned by a faith that should be so freeing!

Remember the song "And They'll Know We Are Christians by Our Love"? Sweatshop Catholics wouldn't make the grade. They don't enjoy life; they endure it. They seem to have forgotten that Jesus was a man of great joy. He went to parties, he ate, laughed, drank, and knew the value of coming together and enjoying life. What has happened to us? Why do we have guilt in our hearts about the good times? Life brings plenty of hardship and pain, so why not live, love, and laugh in the name of Jesus?

In many ways Jesus fulfills the goal of the Consciousness Examen: he is fully aware of the presence of God within and around him. That is what we call full humanity. To walk in his path is to discover the same thing in our lives. The more human we become, the more fully we discover God in our everyday lives. Sweatshop Catholics cannot achieve the fullness of the Consciousness Examen. They still see God as "outside" or "up there" waiting for them to make a mistake.

A Discerning Heart

So how do we become more human? There's no

"humanity diet" or exercise but the reality is rather simple. Life well lived leads to deeper humanity. This is often called a discerning heart. When we live with passion, with love, with tears and with empathy, we touch God in a very deep and beautiful way. The Examen teaches deep living; it teaches living well.

There is a wonderful scene in the Disney classic, *The Lion King*. Simba, the young lion who is to become the next king, is off in the elephant graveyard alone. He is sad about the death of his father, Mufasa and remembers a time when Mufasa promised that he would always be with him. Simba yells out, "You promised me you'd always be with me." In the distance, a wise orangutan named Rafiki hears the cry and comes to Simba. He explains that he knows Mufasa and can lead Simba to him. They travel over mountains and hills and with great anticipation, Simba runs up to the spot where Rafiki points and says, "There is you father." Simba looks down into a still lake and sees his own reflection. Looking back over his shoulder at Rafiki he says in disappointment that it is only his reflection, it is not Mufasa. Rafiki, in his wisdom smiles and simply says, "Look harder." As Simba looks harder, the water stirs and he sees his father's reflection. Rafiki remarks, "You see, he lives in you."

Isn't it the same with God? We need a discerning heart to help us to stop and look. Living life well helps us to look harder; traveling over hills and mountains helps us to look harder. To look deep within is not an easy thing. Like Simba we need others to travel with us and urge us on. No one has cornered the market on the knowledge of God. All of us are apprentices discovering a bit more each day as we stare into the pond of our lives. The examen is the process of looking into that pond and seeing what God has done in our lives. And there is a by-product of this process. It is the recognition of the fact that, "He dwells in you , too!"

So life well lived pushes us to the edge of the pond *and* into the arms of the other. The book of Genesis makes it clear, that we were not meant to be alone. Solitude is nice in the beginning, but eventually, we need to be around people. Christian community is born from this process. This is why we gather together on Sunday, to hear the story, gaze into the pond together and take notice that God lives within each of us individually and collectively.

That is why many theologians call the church the first sacrament. It is in the church that we see the vision of everyone's reflection in the pond and through that reflection we come to see the body of Christ in a new way. Jesus is reflected in the lives of those around us, indeed, "He lives in you"! This is why I have ended every single Sunday homily since I was ordained with the words ". . .to more fully become what we receive from the altar today, the Body of Christ."

If all this is true, and if we take the Examen seriously, we may need to make some changes in our lives. First, people around me are no longer "the enemy" but companions. Second, as we see more clearly into the pond, we change our perspective of people. Third, we desperately and hopelessly need each other.

1. Enemies in Our Midst

This notion is easy to encounter when we do some very

basic human actions like drive the car, wait on line, or even go Christmas shopping! I drive a little over a mile to go to the school where I work. In the short "commute" from the rectory to the school I am amazed by the aggression I encounter. The driving attitude of some people really scares me. Since I also celebrate Mass on Sundays in this rather small town, I must be especially careful of my own driving style. Recently, I accidentally cut someone off at a stop sign. The driver immediately sounded the horn and proudly displayed a hand gesture in my direction. The look on his face was priceless when I caught up to him at the next light, rolled down my window and in full Roman collar, waved and said good morning!

Much the same thing happens after every Sunday Mass as we emerge from the loving and caring atmosphere in church and join the free-for-all in the parking lot. It all seems to be connected to the discernment of spirits that needs to occur in each of our hearts. If you are my companion, you can never be my enemy. We are traveling together; we look out for each other. That is the discernment of the heart that the Consciousness Examen calls us to.

Traveling together also means waiting together. No one in America likes to wait on line. Perhaps the worst place to wait is at the Department of Motor Vehicles. Admittedly better than it was, this is still a trip to purgatory. I usually go with my Walkman on and a pair of rosaries in my pocket. I do this to block out the anger that is all around me while on line. It has made the visits more tolerable. It has also taught me a valuable lesson: namely, that aggression and anger are contagious. We tend to imitate the attitude of the people around us. If we are in an aggressive atmosphere, we will respond aggressively. If we are in a joyful atmosphere, we are much more likely to respond in a like manner.

Think about Disneyworld. It is a disgustingly happy place isn't it? Doesn't everyone smile and smile and smile all day long? Don't we generally follow suit and patiently endure hour-long lines for a four-minute ride? The happiness is contagious. Disneyworld has the secret to successful human living. If you are happy, those around you will generally be the same. This is touching the core of the examen. If we can achieve the knowledge of the presence of God in all we do, our attitude will change radically, others around us will change radically and life as we know it here on the planet Earth will change radically.

The issue of a discerning heart is bigger than Catholicism. It is bigger than all of Christendom. It is an issue of humanity embracing itself and looking out for the other. The simple steps of the Consciousness Examen have led me down the road to achieving a discerning heart. How far down the road depends on the day. As a matter of fact, once you come to know your discerning heart— once you encounter God's radical presence in the world—it gets a bit tougher to sit back and see injustice and poverty around us. This is primarily because through the grace of God, we have been given a taste of what could be. Once you encounter this, you're compelled to action, to reach out to the needy and to cherish the present. At the same time, this can lead to frustration because our mission is not complete. There is work to be done in God's vineyard!

2. A Change of Perspective

Seeing what can be and knowing that God is in our everyday existence lead to a change of perspective. Basically there are two levels of this new perspective: a change of my self view, and a change of my view of others. I am no longer insignificant if I am in a place where the spirit of God dwells. I am a missionary. I can make a difference. Conversely, if I do not participate fully in life, love and laughter, I am missed.

I have a very hard time remembering the early days of my priesthood. They were tumultuous days filled with effort and anxiety. One helpful thing I did in my early priesthood was to keep a file in which I placed all the letters of thanks and support that I received from parishioners. I figured, when I was down, I would need to look at these letters to remember that I was loved, and that I made a difference. You know, I never looked at the file once! Why? I didn't need it. I knew I was loved and I knew I made a difference by the ongoing support I experienced from the people around me.

My perspective changed. I was less frail than I thought. Through the grace of God, I had learned the first change of perspective necessary for a discerning heart—I made a difference.

How does one achieve this? Actually, I don't think it is a milestone one achieves, it's more like a fluid life process that constantly needs work and reflection. I have bouts of insecurity, particularly in relation to knowing that I am lovable and loved. It seems to me that original sin is somehow connected to not loving oneself enough. Somehow, we "dysfunctionally" love ourselves. It takes work to change our perspective.

It seems that when we accept our own incompleteness, we can accept the incompleteness of the rest of the world. There is a process here. It calls us to tolerance and acceptance. It calls us to let go of our anger and frustration and embrace the incompleteness of our boss, our spouse, our parent. Remember, they are probably doing the same thing with you!

Remember the old song, "What's the Matter With Kids Today":

"Why can't they be like we are, perfect in every way?
What's the matter with kids today?"

We are all incomplete and striving to become more of who we have been called to be. It's hard to accept the shortcomings of the ones we love and even harder to accept the shortcomings of the ones we don't! Think about the person who all but runs you off the road. Our first thought is that he or she is a jerk. We may even be tempted to catch up to them and let them know that they cannot get away with this. Or what about the person who cuts you on line in a store? Cutting didn't end in grade school; it still drives humanity nuts! Or the obnoxious neighbor who uses your driveway for U-turns? These moments need us to step back and remember that humanity is not perfect, but charity can prevail!

Some people are real challenges. They are the "challenge of the missionaries." To work with them and not imitate their aggression, we need a change of perspective. This is not easy but God calls us to look for the small victories. St. Paul tells us that our "attitude must be Christ's." There lies the heart of the matter. A missionary spirit needs the heart of Jesus which accepted people where they were without condemnation. I find it interesting that Jesus never said, "why can't you be like me?" I guess he knew us too well. We cannot achieve full humanity until we can recognize its brokenness and even rejoice in it. We do pretty well for such a motley crew! This leads us to the third point.

3. A Hopeless Need for Each Other

We hopelessly need each other. A discerning heart readily admits this. I like to think I am on the road to a discerning heart, but this particular notion is difficult for me. Not only must I believe I make a difference, but I must admit that I need others and that others need me.

Let's start with the easier of the two. It is easier for us to accept the fact, even relish the fact that we are needed. Our kids need us, our spouses need us, our friends need us. Everyone likes to be needed. Actually, it is often the source of great disappointment to parents when they are no longer needed in the same way by their growing son or daughter. This should be a source of encouragement not discouragement. If we believed in our goodness we could embrace the fact that we did the best we could given our gifts and abilities. Instead, we worry, we angst, we get into therapy, we become resentful, we stop communicating, we hurt. There is never a time when our kids don't need us. The needs change, but there is a need. I need my parents in my life in a different way now then when I was 17, but I still need them.

It is beautiful to see the network of people who need us. Spouses need each other in different ways at different times in their lives. Friends need our support and need our honesty. We find it difficult at times to challenge those we love but that is part of being needed, calling them to more.

We have a wonderful example in the life of Jesus. He constantly fulfills a need for others by challenging and healing. I used to have an impression of Jesus as a controlling person, always pointing out the faults of others. That's because I didn't like to have my faults pointed out. I still don't! But those we love need our wisdom and our perspective on life.

Sometimes just being there with someone can make all the difference in the world. As a priest, that is my big secret. Just being there. For all of us, there are occasions when we feel quite inadequate. Death, sickness, wakes, hospitals. I dislike them all. Put me in a hospital and my skin begins to crawl. However, my ministry often brings me to these moments. I used to worry about what to say. Some of my mentors have passed on the secret: just be there.

I can remember one of the first funeral Masses I celebrated. It was for an elderly gentleman who died of cancer. His wife was there along with their three adult children and assorted grandchildren. I was petrified in the sacristy before the Mass. I hardly knew how to do the ritual of incensing the body, I didn't know how to "work" the prayer book on the altar, and, it was ninety degrees in the church. Seeing my nervousness, the sexton put on a bevy of fans to keep me from sweating profusely during the Mass. While I was incensing the body after the offertory of the Mass, the fans blew the pages in the Sacramentary on the altar. I didn't notice this when I came back, and proceeded to read the prayer . . . "Lord, we thank you for the gift of your servant, John, who served us so dutifully as pope."

I couldn't believe what I was reading. Did I really just say this out loud? Just two pages flipped and I was on the page that was the funeral mass for the pope! I tried to recoup, "He was like a pope to us because he led our family." Nice try, but too late. The family realized what had happened and went hysterical. The leader of song ran from the sanctuary screaming in laughter. All I could do was join in! After the Mass, the wife told me that it was one of the most beautiful experiences of her life. She said it was because this celebration, though sad, was a celebration of life, love and laughter (my words, not hers). I still see that woman, and laugh with her every time I speak to her!

People need us to laugh and cry with them. What about us? Do we need anyone? Have we "come into this world alone and intend to go back the same way"? I hate that line. I don't believe we go home alone. We go home carrying all the love that we received from others, and that love takes many forms. With all the personality studies that are now in vogue, you would think that some pop psychologist would develop a "loner" personality trait. Yet there is none. No personality is a "loner." To be a person is to be in relationship. But to admit relationship is difficult. It involves vulnerability—putting our hearts on the line—and that is often a scary thing.

No one likes to be vulnerable in love or in everyday life. I am not a big fan of asking for directions. I'll find a place myself, thank you. I have a wonderful secretary who gets directions for my various speaking engagements, and from there, I am on my own. I always give myself extra time, because no matter how good the directions are, I inevitably end up lost and late. If I asked for directions as soon as I was lost, I would be where I was expected early every time. But seeking help implies vulnerability. It asserts the fact that we aren't perfect.

Our neediness is complex. Ever try to get over a flu without a doctor? It can be done, but it takes a lot longer! Ever try to get by in life without being loved, touched, cared for, embraced, kissed, hugged, treated like a king or a queen? I propose it cannot be done. We need love. We need to be told "I love you." It's odd, but as I get older, I need to be loved more. Maybe that is the gift of age: interdependence vs. independence.

I have friends that I love as much as I can love who have a difficult time loving back. I know the struggle; I feel the void. But I have come to see that the loving takes on different forms. They love differently than I love. We need to acknowledge the complex ways in which love is expressed. A discerning heart can acknowledge that. We are different in our gifts, we express ourselves in different ways. But the reality that we need each other remains. I wince at interviews of the rich and famous where they proclaim themselves "self-made." Kind of God-like isn't it! Not one of us is self made; all of us are made through a complex maze of triumph and tragedy that has led us to who we are at this moment.

My mother often sends me "thinking of you" cards. I see my parents most Sunday afternoons and speak to my parents during the week, yet I still get a card every couple of weeks. I love that! I can even admit, I need that! They are a part of who I am and I need reminders of that all the time.

Look around your home today. Is it filled with stories and memories—a gathering of life, love and laughter? I remember visiting a family for dinner a few years back. Their living room was a sea of pictures of their three children that traced their lives from infancy to adulthood. Our homes should tell a story. I believe that is why it is so moving to go to the Holy Land or to Rome or to Assisi. To visit a place which is part of our history can be a moving experience. This can happen when we visit the "old neighborhood" too! The "holy" places on earth tell the story of holy people. Even if we don't know exactly where their nativities, crosses and resurrections are, being in the place makes us part of the story.

To allow ourselves to be loved is to allow ourselves to become part of someone else's story, and we in turn become a part of theirs. This is the key to human intimacy. Just visiting someone's home helps that process. My home tells the story of my being loved, and everywhere you look are memories of the people who God put in my life. For my money, that's more important than any interior decorator's plan!

There is another important component to all of this—vulnerability. I don't mind knowing in my heart that I am vulnerable, but "laying it on the line" with someone else is very scary. There is a line ingrained in my mind from the musical "Carnival" where one of the characters using a puppet of a lion says, "Do you think that if I get pricked, I do not bleed?" Even lions bleed. Jesus bleeds. The Gospels are quite emphatic about that. To love means you could end up bleeding, bruised and battered.

Humanity is caught up with vulnerability. In most families, when someone dies, their jewelry and other possessions are divided up among the surviving family members and friends. When my Nana died, I asked for one thing from her: her wooden spoon. When she used the wooden spoon to stir the sauce she taught me about life, love, and laughter. Every time I use it, I think of her. My aunt got her china cabinet. But grandpa put all of the china that we used each holiday in big boxes, wrapped in newspaper. He hid them away in his attic, so the pieces would not get broken. My aunt put the empty china cabinet in her dining room, and every time we went to her house after Nana died, I had tears in my eyes looking into it. The first Christmas after Nana died we went to Aunt Mary's house for Christmas dinner. It was a sad one, but we found strength in coming together. As I went into the dining room, I saw Nana's empty china cabinet. On the table were plastic dishes and utensils. It made me sad to see this. Christmas wasn't the same without Nana's china on the table. Life is meant to be lived. China is meant to be used. If it gets broken, that's part of why it exists.

We are called by God to use the best of ourselves to love. The temptation is to use only the "safe" part of our emotional life, but the vulnerable part of us, our deepest selves is the only way to true joy and meaning. Most of us learn through experience that if we really love, we're likely to get chipped, or even broken in the process. Look at Jesus' life. I still think it's better than life in a china cabinet.

So let us begin. Let's look at these five steps; open yourself to the Spirit. Matthew ends his Gospel with Jesus sending his disciples forth to continue his missionary work. In many ways we are sent too. We are called to become his body and live his word. Allow the words of Jesus to speak to you in a new way:

> "All power in heaven and on earth has been given to me. Go, therefore, and make disciples of all nations, baptizing them in the name of the Father, and of the Son, and of the holy Spirit, teaching them to observe all that I have commanded you. And behold, I am with you always, until the end of the age."
>
> MATTHEW 28:18-20

~ 3 ~

The First Step:
A Prayer for Enlightenment

ALL THE WORLD dislikes a know-it-all. Remember the last time you were in the presence of a know-it-all; the tendency is to tune them out. Trouble is almost every family has a know-it-all. They are the ones who know the best ways to get somewhere, where you could have gotten "it" cheaper, and will offer you the latest health and fitness advice while they smoke a huge cigar. Then there are Religious know-it-alls. At one time I thought these people were sort of enlightened—like mystics. They knew God, they knew it all, had all the answers. I think I was wrong about most of them.

What I've learned is that there are very few things that we need to know and actually I got a great insight about this while interviewing a potential theology teacher for our school. One of the questions I always ask is, "What do you consider to be the most important issue in the Church today?" Her answer was, "The Church needs mystics." She elaborated that in her view, a mystic was an enlightened person who knew the presence of God in his or her everyday life. She also said that this is what the Church needs its priests to be. Amen to that!

Spirituality is deeply connected with mysticism; that is, knowing the presence of God in our everyday lives. The first step of the Consciousness Examen is the prayer for enlightenment. It boils down to this: we spend a moment asking God for a "eureka" moment. Enlightenment is something that is hard to grasp. It can't be bought, you can't write away for it, and, when you get right down to it, you can't even search for it. It just happens. For some it is the loss of innocence about life. When it does happen in some small or large way we are never the same again. It becomes the way to holiness and deeper union with God and affords us the opportunity to mature spiritually. We need it in order to cope and live in faith. Religious education may have formally ended after our confirmation, but the learning—the enlightening—doesn't end until we're in the funeral home!

Webster's dictionary defines enlightenment as "having knowledge and spiritual insight." If you read on you will see my favorite definition: "an educated guess or informed opinion." Here is a definition I can live with! An enlightened spirituality is not one that has all the answers, or even knows all the questions. It basically boils down to this: to be enlightened or in the process of enlightenment involves the desire to get into the wrestling ring with God. Allow me to explain.

I love watching "religious television." Our local cable system carries our diocesan television station, "Telicare," while also carrying religious programming from around the nation. Often the interviewers and the guests seem to have it all together, and try to get across to the rest of us the key to spirituality. Once in a while I'd like to see someone interviewed who is like me; sometimes confused, sometimes lost, and yet sometimes remarkably together! "Public" spirituality is often about answered prayers, not the struggle with the unanswered ones. No one likes to hear about a family that prays for a sick child who dies. Yet, that is life. People die, prayers seem to fall on deaf ears; we question, and yet we walk in faith.

That's why I think spirituality is like wrestling with God. It's not that God is trying to beat us. It is an interior struggle which involves our hearts, minds and souls struggling to make sense out of life and love. If you're the kind of person (like me) who likes closure, neatness, and all the ducks in a row, this is difficult business.

It's like having company. When someone is coming over to the house, we throw all the junk in the nearest closet, shut the door, spray air freshener and hope for the best. I have a confession to make. I am a medicine cabinet snoop. Open someone's medicine cabinet and their world is at your fingertips! You can learn a lot from a medicine cabinet: habits, neatness, illness—they're full of information! Over the years I've seen the neatest and the most untidy medicine cabinets. Being a medicine cabinet snoop, I always keep mine ready for inspection. My mess is hidden somewhere else!

We need to acknowledge "the mess" as we pray for enlightenment. For some of us, enlightenment comes on the mountainside while sipping iced tea, for others, it is in the struggle, in the wrestling that we become *enlightened*—able to make an *informed decision*, an *educated guess* about God in our lives.

Knowing another's struggle and journey to enlightenment can truly be a source of inspiration and can literally fuel our own prayer for enlightenment. When I was just beginning to study philosophy, we were assigned a classic book on epistemology. It was called *Insight*, and it was written by a famous Jesuit scholar, Father Bernard Lonergan. I spent a year of my life studying page after page of this book and felt quite close to this great scholar. I remember sitting in class daydreaming of what "the great Lonergan" might look like, very serious and stern, like someone with all the answers.

One autumn, a small group of us decided to take a road trip to Boston. Basically, it was a free trip; we'd stay at their seminary and eat their food, so it was perfect for college students without jobs! Anyway, I found out that Fr. Lonergan lived on the grounds of Boston College, right next to the seminary. I told my friends that I was going to call him and see if we could meet him and have him sign our books. They cynically said, "He'd never see us, we're college kids, not scholars." Well, sure enough, I called and Father Lonergan said he'd meet us the next evening at the priest's residence. I remember going to the front door, nervous and concerned that I didn't remember all of his teachings, thinking this was a mistake and I was an idiot for trying to talk with a genius like Lonergan. After I rang the bell, my friends and I waited until the door was opened by a little old man with thick glasses, a flannel shirt, khaki pants and a little crop of white hair. I said that we were here to see Father Lonergan, thinking to myself, isn't it great that they gave a job to this nice old man. He quickly answered, "You found him, who are you?" This was a grandfather, wise and learned, with many stories to tell.

He spent hours telling us stories of his life, triumphs and tragedies, and of his illness that ultimately would call him home to God. We never once talked about *Insight* or any other philosophy. After he signed our books, we left. Interestingly, we were all elated, uplifted, yes, *enlightened* by being in his presence—more than any discussion of his work could achieve. I knew more about God after being with him. What was his secret?

The secret was enlightenment. He had reflected on his life and shared some of his conclusions with us through stories and anecdotes. He made the connections between God and his life; he knew the power of the Spirit. That is what the first stage of the Consciousness Examen is all about. A prayer for enlightenment is a prayer to make "God-connections" so that we may continue to wrestle with God in our lives. I often speak about prayer and spirituality in terms of a wrestling ring. Enlightenment doesn't seem to come during peaceful times; it seems to come through our struggle and inner turmoil.

I can barely remember anything from my first years of ordination. They are a blur. Actually, they were a struggle to find God in a new and exciting way. Every time I celebrated a sacrament in those early days as a priest, a remarkable amount of energy came out of me. I remember celebrating Mass and needing a nap afterwards! Looking back, it was a wrestling match. It was a struggle between my insignificance and unworthiness and my desire to be my best; between my mixed motives; between my God and me. Though difficult, those years were ones of tremendous growth. Throughout our lives, enlightenment seems to follow the struggle. No one knows what it is like to be married until they are married, no one knows what it is like to be a parent until they are a parent, and no one knows what it is to love until they love.

To experience enlightenment is to experience love. When we fall in love with someone we see them in a new light, they are totally new to us. Think about it. There is that wonderful moment when we think to ourselves, "My God, I am in love with this person!" That is a moment of enlightenment. It's something we have to come to, it's the educated guess of how we feel about the person. We cannot prove it, we cannot stop it or prevent it, but we know when it is there. It touches the Holy, the Enlightened. Our flame touches the eternal flame. Great moment, yet not without struggle, wonder and awe. It is participating in love with a capital "L."

We love our children. Yet there comes a time when we know them in a way that is different from when they were young. I remember when I was a freshman at St. John the Baptist Diocesan High School. I tried out for freshman football. Not because I thought I could play football, but I thought that was what my dad wanted from his son. My coach, Walter Lace (my dear friend and associate at St. John's now!) worked us hard the first day. As we finished the day he told us to run a mile and then go home. I thought I would die! I began to run the mile and before long I was the only one running. I remember well that everything in me hurt, and I knew well that I would never be an athlete. (Actually, I knew this from early in my life, but I wanted my Dad to be proud of me.) Barely able to walk, on the last lap around, I noticed that my Dad was standing on the side watching me finish. All the other kids had finished and were walking toward their cars with their parents and there was my Dad, watching his overweight, artistic and creative son trying to be an athlete. I'll never forget the finish line. He came over, put his arm around me and said, "Let's go home, you don't ever have to do this again for me. I love you just the way you are." Amen!

I think my Dad and I were both enlightened that day. We made a new discovery: who I was was fine with Dad and I could finally work on being who I was, not who I wanted to be for someone else. I really believe that moment had a lot to do with my vocation and my spiritual life today. I learned, in the wrestling ring of the football field, that I was O.K. as I was. God makes us different; different gifts, same spirit. Start celebrating those gifts!

That is true enlightenment; when we come to recognize something new about ourselves, our God or another. We leave the moment different than when we came to the moment. Movies do it, books do it, plays do it, liturgy does it, and they do it most effectively when they touch the chord of love within each of us.

I went to the Holocaust Museum in Washington, DC recently. I meandered in, hot and bothered with the summer heat. I expected to learn something and see some artifacts. In actuality, I encountered the horror of the holocaust head-on and left a different person—enlightened by the experience. I remember going through that museum trying to hide my tears, but then I noticed that I was not alone. In fact, many people were in solidarity with me. There was a strength in human empathy that helped me to feel hope in the midst of tragedy. I believe this experience led to further enlightenment for me.

Enlightenment never ends. It keeps going and going! Healing, love, and passion are the things that we are made of and these moments are the moments that lead to enlightenment.

Think of the life of Jesus. In John's Gospel Jesus speaks to the disciple he loved from the cross, "There is your mother" and to the his mother, "There is your son." On the cross, Jesus comes to enlightenment himself. Jesus had the wherewithal to entrust them to each other—to enlighten them—so that they might care for each other forever.

Jesus is famous for his ability to enlighten others. The Gospels are full of examples of Jesus bringing people to a new moment in their lives. Let's look at three such moments to illustrate the importance of enlightenment in the life of Jesus and to give us a foundation for our prayer of enlightenment.

1. *Jesus enlightens by healing people in sin.* Time and time again throughout the Gospels Jesus' healing touch brings people to new understandings of themselves. Recount the story of the woman caught in the act of adultery. Jesus brings her to a new level of understanding herself. She is a sinner, but she is forgiven; go and avoid this sin in the future. Catching somebody in the act is always sweet. Jesus could have said, "Ha, I got you!" Instead, he forgives and sends her away a new person. Think about it. Do you think she committed that sin again? I think she avoided it; I think her life was changed. Sometimes it is when we are caught red handed that the Lord breaks in and gives us the grace of enlightenment.

I remember being on vacation on the east end of Long Island. Actually, a priest friend and I were working at a "nun camp." This is a place where women Religious go to spend a week of vacation sponsored by their order. Anyway, I was driving along the road, and noticed in my rear-view mirror a police car following me. I immediately checked my speedometer and confirmed that I was going exactly 55 miles an hour; not a mile over, not a mile under. Within minutes, the lights were on and I was being pulled over. I was a bit irritated because the police were known to pull over "tourists" for the slightest infraction. After giving the officer my license and registration, he asked, "Do you know how fast you were going?" I quickly responded, "As a matter of fact, I do. I was going 55, not a mile over, not a mile under." He responded, "You're right, you were going exactly 55, but in a 30 mile-an-hour zone!"

Sometimes death is easier than life! He caught me. My friend suggested he arrest me for my behavior but the officer laughed and went back to his car scratching his head. I left enlightened; I never drive in that area without diligently checking my speed.

Getting caught isn't all that bad. It's sometimes part of the road to holiness. On this level, the prayer for enlightenment is a prayer to be "caught" that we may be brought to deeper holiness. It sounds a bit scary, but believe me it works!

2. *Jesus enlightens by raising the dead.* Jesus' raising of the dead always intrigued me. Jesus sees a poor widow who has lost her only son. He is moved by her tears and raises him from the dead. Imagine the faces on the people who witnessed that event! Where is the intrigue?

Raised to die again? Why? Well, I think it has to do with enlightenment. After that event, people had to notice that death could not hold a grip on them. They, too, would live and die on a deeper level. They died enlightened, and so did everyone they knew.

Anyone who has walked someone through sickness to death knows firsthand the enlightenment that deep Christ-like healing affords. Over the summer I was asked to go to the bedside of a man who was suffering with cancer. As I arrived at the house I was struck by all of the cars on the street. Inside was his entire family, surrounding his bedside and praying with him. As we talked, he thanked his family for all their love and support. They told him how much they loved him. I anointed him in the name of Jesus. A few days later, I visited him again. He was clearly close to eternal life. We gathered again, his family again telling him how much they loved him. Although he could not speak, his eyes told the story of love, of farewell, and of his deep faith. Eugene died a few hours later. Through the power of Jesus, his family raised him from the dead. They literally loved him to life with Jesus. He died a man of enlightenment. The great part is that he shared that enlightenment with his loving family and with me. I hope that when it's my time to go home, I will know so much love!

3. *Jesus enlightens when he eats with people.* Sharing a meal is a holy thing. Whenever Jesus is sharing a meal, he is in the process of bringing people to a new level. I love the feeding of the five thousand. Jesus is on the mountainside; he has gathered the masses; they are hungry. I remember one scripture scholar in the seminary

explaining that perhaps the miracle lay in the fact that the five thousand individuals that day were so interconnected through Jesus that they were moved to share what they had stashed under their cloaks with each other.

That is true enlightenment—strangers recognizing that they are brothers and sisters. Imagine walking down the street in a major city, breaking a Big Mac in half and giving half to a stranger. Not only do they take it graciously, but they give you half of their slice of pizza. Enlightening? I think so.

My radio ministry brings me to many rock concerts, both as spectator and interviewer. I remember three young girls offering me some of their French fries at one concert. They were soaked in ketchup, and the girls were eating them with their fingers. I immediately said no thanks and thought how disgusting the idea was. Then I got to thinking. This concert had created a sense of unity among the crowd. I remember being distracted and thinking to myself, "Eat the fries, *share the meal* you jerk!" After about twenty minutes of reflection, I tapped one of them on the shoulder and said, "Can I try some now?" They were glad to oblige and probably didn't think twice about the experience, but I had been enlightened. It was the miracle on the mountainside all over again. It was Jesus telling me, if you share, if you care, you'll never be hungry.

Jesus calls us to enlightenment through healing, through raising the dead, and sharing a meal. It is integral to the Consciousness Examen to begin here, with a prayer for a new understanding. Without enlightenment, we cannot really know the intense presence of

Jesus in the world. We will miss it. The opposite of *enlighten* is *darken* or *confuse*. That is the option! To live in the light or to live in the dark; to understand or to confuse.

Jesus constantly accuses the Pharisees and Sadducees of blindness and confusion. That is typical of the person who does not pursue enlightenment. They get stuck in rules, in rubrics, and in "tradition." The Church is a gathering of people who celebrate faith, who live together, work together, laugh together, cry together, and even die together. That's what Jesus encourages us to do when he washes the disciples' feet. Perhaps this is the single greatest example of enlightenment in the life of Jesus:

> ". . .during supper, fully aware that the Father had put everything into his power and that he had come from God and was returning to God, he rose from supper and took off his outer garments. He took a towel and tied it around his waist. Then he poured water into a basin and began to wash the disciples' feet and dry them with the towel around his waist. He came to Simon Peter, who said to him, "Master, are you going to wash my feet?" Jesus answered and said to him, "What I am doing, you do not understand now, but you will understand later." Peter said to him, "You will never wash my feet." Jesus answered him, "Unless I wash you, you will have no inheritance with me." Simon Peter said to him, "Master, then not only my feet, but my hands and head as well." Jesus said to him, "Whoever has bathed has no need except to have his feet washed, for he is clean all over; so you are clean. . .when he had washed their feet [and] put

his garments back on and reclined at table again, he said to them, "Do you realize what I have done for you? You call me 'teacher' and 'master,' and rightly so, for indeed I am. If I, therefore, the master and teacher, have washed your feet, you ought to wash one another's feet. I have given you a model to follow, so that as I have done for you, you should also do. Amen, amen, I say to you, no slave is greater than his master nor any messenger greater than the one who sent him. If you understand this, blessed are you if you do it.

JOHN 13:2-17

Blessed will we be if we do it. We will be holy if we see with new vision, life will have deeper meaning through washing one another's feet—through seeing one another as holy, valuable, and irreplaceable. Indeed this is an important first step. It thrusts us into the missionary work of Jesus and into the arms of one another. Now that is something worth praying for!

~ 4 ~

The Second Step:
Reflective Thanksgiving

"All good gifts around us are sent from heaven above, so
thank the Lord, oh thank the Lord for all his love...."
"All Good Gifts" from *Godspell*

I REMEMBER my seventh grade religious education
teacher, Sister Raymond telling us that the most important prayer we could ever pray was to thank God for
everything we have in our lives. At the time I had a sister dying of leukemia; I didn't have enough toys and
attention; and I couldn't for the life of me think of anything I'd like to thank God for. I could think of plenty
that I'd like to ask for, but to thank Him for—nothing.

My reaction was probably very common and that's
why Sister mentioned it in class. We are the "want more"
people. Get a new car, look for a better one; get a raise,
want another; buy one CD, want fifty more. It never
ends! Consumerism is very American! Don't get me
wrong, I am not one of those who ascribes to the "leave
everything and follow me" theology. We have things; we
struggle with the *thingdom* versus the *kingdom*. There

must be a way to own things and still be kingdom people. I think of the story of the rich young man in Mark's Gospel:

> Jesus said to him, "If you wish to be perfect, go, sell what you have and give to [the] poor, and you will have treasure in heaven. Then come, follow me." When the young man heard this statement, he went away sad, for he had many possessions. Then Jesus said to his disciples, "Amen, I say to you, it will be hard for one who is rich to enter the kingdom of heaven."
>
> MATTHEW 19:21-23

Good news for all of us. It is not impossible to enter the kingdom, just hard! In some ways those who have less have it easier. For us it is harder, but not impossible. Good news indeed!

The Good News starts with the second step of the Consciousness Examen, a moment of reflective thanksgiving. It involves spending some moments thanking God for His wonders in our lives, and the many gifts we have received through His grace and love. That's the starting point for combating our "thingdom." It's God who provides the gifts; we don't earn them. Can we celebrate the gifts we have instead of focussing on the ones we don't?

What is your most valuable possession; the house, the car, the Hummels, the Lladro collection? Look at how St. Paul begins his letter to the Phillipians:

> I give thanks to my God at every remembrance of you, praying always with joy in my every prayer for all of

you, because of your partnership for the gospel from the
first day until now.

Phillipians 1:3-5

It is indeed true that our greatest possession is the gift
of the people in our lives. A week doesn't go by at St.
John the Baptist Diocesan High School that I don't get
asked the age old question to priests, "How can you live
without a family?"

I always answer that question by saying that I do
indeed have a family; it just depends on how you define
a family. I have wonderful parents, caring relatives, un-
believably supportive friends, and a wonderful ex-
tended family, namely the people of God. You can live
without a wife, husband, or children. However, you cannot survive alone. *People who need people, are the luckiest
people in the world!* There lies the treasure.

I am really amazed at how often we take the people
who love us for granted. I remember going on retreat for
thirty days of silence. Solitude is not my gift, nor is
silence! The thought of being away from my family and
friends for thirty days was quite debilitating to say the
least! I remember going over this again and again in my
mind and finally deciding to make a list of everyone I
love and take it with me. I began to write their names
and as the list grew I was amazed at all of the people
God had put into my life. I took the list with me and
added to it each day, and by the thirtieth day, the list was
remarkably long and took up over two spiral notebooks!
I still have those notebooks; they're a great reminder to
me of how blessed I am.

In the early days of religious formation, close friendships were discouraged; they were called PFs—particular friends. People were to avoid these kinds of close, intimate relationships. In a sense this was in contradiction to the life of Jesus that all of us, ordained or not, are called to emulate. Jesus had PFs; he had friends that everyone knew he loved. There was one, John, who shared a rather public intimacy with him. In John's Gospel we see that Jesus was grateful to God for the "ones he gave him in this life." Intimacy, love, and friendship were not something to avoid; they were something to be grateful for.

Our lives are blessed too, with wonderful spouses, amazing children, and friends who are like family to us. Most people are lucky enough to go through life with some people who love them no matter what. The line from *It's a Wonderful Life* rings true: "No [one] is poor who has friends."

It seems that it is around the table that we celebrate these people. We gather night after night as a family to share a meal; we invite friends over to share a meal with us; we dine at a restaurant to celebrate special occasions with people we love. Eating is an important part of thankfulness! It puts us in a spirit of gratitude. That's why the gathering at Sunday Mass is so important to us. We gather around our parish table and hear God's word and break bread as we work (that's what the word *liturgy* means) at being thankful for each other. That process is the second step of the Examen. A prayer for thankfulness can be done in front of the bathroom mirror while brushing your teeth, but thankfulness reaches its apex at the parish table, as we gather together to become what we receive. The more thankful we are—the closer we are to becoming the body of Christ.

This concept is so meaningful to me that I had the line, "And in the end, the love you take is equal to the love you make" inscribed on my chalice. This quote is not from the Scriptures, it is from the last line of the last song of the Beatles' last album, *Abbey Road*. If you love small, if you hold back on loving, that will be your experience of love. Our goal is to give all of ourselves in love to each other as Jesus did.

I admit, although this is a meaningful line, it is an odd inscription for a chalice! I'll never forget a Bishop in our diocese using my chalice for a confirmation Mass. I could see him looking at the engraving during the Mass, and afterwards he told me it was very interesting and asked where was it from. I nervously told him it was a proverb from an obscure part of the Old Testament, and that he'd probably never seen it! He bought it and I was relieved!

Regardless of where I got it, this line has helped me much of my life. If we are a grateful people, we will receive the same. I have found this to be true again and again. God loves us so much that we are called to do the same. The more we love and live in thankfulness, the closer we become to what we receive from the altar.

I remember meeting Paul McCartney, my favorite Beatle, and telling him and his wife about using that special line on my chalice. I told him that I believed the line was truly inspired, and that it was a way of life for me since my childhood. He looked at his wife Linda and said, "Now I've heard everything!" We spoke about love and thankfulness and wherever these two dwelled, there was God. I didn't know at the time that his wife was terminally ill with cancer. Perhaps our meeting and brief discussion made Paul's lyrics even more meaningful for his wife and him. I was standing in the front row during his concert that evening. He looked at me, winked and said, "These words are important for all of us who try to love well." He began a song called, "Hope of Deliverance" *(from the darkness that surrounds us)*. Paul was on to it. He knew that the more you love like God, the happier you will be. It was the root of his life—why he could remain married for over twenty years, and why he could live in faith as he carried his wife back to God in love and thanksgiving.

We are called to a life stance of thanksgiving. Recognizing that when push comes to shove everything is a gift, is where it's at. In the context of the Examen, this is the second of five moments of reflection. In reality a big part of gratefulness involves using our gifts to help others. Our diocese uses a program called "Stewardship" which enforces the premise that we have been blessed by God and are called to share time, talent, and treasure with each other. Using our gifts well is in itself a way of giving thanks.

Reflect for a moment on the three areas in the Stewardship program—time, talent, and treasure. In reality, we spend very little time being thankful for time. We are all so busy; it is difficult to think of ourselves as blessed with time. Once after a wonderful day of pumpkin picking with some friends, we were very quiet in the car on the way home. I think it was because it was a time of gratitude for a great day spent with friends. When we allow God to enter our time, it is a mini-incarnation of sorts and our time with family and friends becomes a time graced by God. The same is true for the use of all our gifts.

Each of us has gifts to share. We have heard that a hundred times but I wonder how many people truly believe it. The young people that I see everyday have trouble seeing their gifts and all of us suffer with a lack of understanding in regard to our gifts. It is impossible to be grateful for gifts that we don't know we have! The Examen helps to unveil our gifts in such a way that they become a treasure in our lives. We are called to love ourselves, so that we may love others. Remember the Beatles: the love you take equals the love you make. Jesus said, "where your treasure is, there also will your heart be" (Matthew 6:21). A thankful heart is rooted in the treasures of our lives. This reaches far beyond our "net worth" to our most valuable possessions, namely, the people we love.

Stewardship and thanksgiving are intimately connected. To truly pray a prayer of thanksgiving, we have to be stewards of creation, and perhaps more importantly good stewards of our lives!

Thanksgiving for the Cross

I still remember the day like it was yesterday. I was called out of my eighth grade class to the principal's office. As I walked down the hallway, tears began to fall down my cheeks. Inside his office, I saw my father and one of his dear friends with tears in their eyes. They didn't say much. I knew what had happened; my sister had died of leukemia. She had been sick for three years, and spent much of the last year at the hospital. In the early 1970s there was little hope for acute lymphatic leukemia; there were no bone marrow transplants, very little aggressive chemotherapy, and ultimately, very little chance of survival. It was a sad story, the saddest chapter of my life. There were no bereavement groups at that time, and no organized support for families who have lost a child. My family and I were truly lost. Many of our relatives and friends didn't know what to say or do; some withdrew. I went back to school after a few days, and tried to act like nothing happened. If I was asked then what redemptive value my sister's death would have in my life, I couldn't have told you. It was senseless, without justification, particularly from a God who was supposed to be love.

As I look back now, I see value in the horrible pain my family endured. We learned a lot about independence and interdependence, and perhaps most importantly, we learned about faith. We learned first-hand the faith of Mary holding her dead son, the faith of Lazarus' sisters and the faith of the father who approached Jesus and said, "My little daughter is dead."

It is true that the experience of death changes someone forever. My sister's death has helped me to understand myself, and to serve Jesus through serving those in sorrow. Many of the funerals that I am asked to celebrate are tragic. They involve young people, young parents, all called home at a time that seems too soon. I have found that my experience of sorrow and suffering has helped me to be effective at these times. I feel very comfortable with the siblings of the deceased person. I know the pain and disbelief that comes with tragic death.

Somehow, this all connects to an odd sort of thanksgiving: thanksgiving for the cross. All of the struggle, pain, and tragedy in our lives, if recognized, can be a source of God's presence to us. Think of a time in your life when you didn't know where to turn. If you're like most of us, you turned to God. At times of the cross we are led by God to God. God draws near in tragedy. Actually, the immanence of God in human tragedy is awe-inspiring.

There are many books in theology written about God's immanence and transcendence, i.e., God is intensely near and close, yet impossible to encounter fully.

I prefer to think of immanence in terms of two friends I recently married. To the world outside of their family and friends, they are just a couple, but to those who know them they are deeply in love. That's the difference with immanence. To know intuitively, immanently, is to know what others could easily miss. Pile thirty thousand people into a stadium for a ballgame, it is hard to know who is in love, who is suffering, who is lonely and unfulfilled. Immanence involves an intimate knowledge of someone. That's why relationships are so special to us. When we get to know someone, we touch something more. Yet we never know everything about that person. Even a spouse of fifty years can surprise us!

Psychologists tell us that a human suffers most greatly from two realities: death and separation. When a relationship changes through divorce, we experience death. The response is often deep-rooted anger that takes its toll physically, emotionally and spiritually. It is impossible to just sweep this pain away. For awhile nothing can really make us feel better. Faith, time, and hope are the best answers for those of us walking through the desert of divorce.

When a son or daughter moves away, we experience a type of death. This can happen with our parents as well. My parents spend the winter months in Florida, and though I am very happy that they can enjoy their retirement together, the separation is difficult. Separation causes a void which needs to be filled.

I know many people who spend a great deal of time and energy trying to fill the hole with all the wrong things: power, prestige, club activities, alcohol, exercise, food, even over-involvement in Church. Most spiritual writers say that we have to become comfortable with the hole that ultimately cannot be filled except by God.

I like to think that the Spirit of God can take the hole in our hearts and fill it with love. Not the love of the movies or a novel, but the love which embraces loss and separation and says, you are not alone I am with you. Even on the cross of your life, I am with you. As a priest for ten years, I have never celebrated any other Holy Week Liturgy but Good Friday. Every time it came up in a planning meeting, I always got assigned Good Friday.

At first I thought this was odd, even a bit unfair, to never sing the great opening line of the Easter Vigil, "Christ Our Light." But in reflection, maybe this is how God wants it to be for me now. I have come to know Him in suffering and in loss, and have turned out to be a person of hope. Good Friday is always a preparation for the celebration of the resurrection. It is here that our suffering makes sense and here that we find hope for the holes in our soul.

Thanksgiving for the Resurrection

No moment of reflective thanksgiving can really be complete without a moment of gratitude for the effect of the resurrection on our lives. This event has changed our history forever. We share life, love and laughter; we suffer and live in confusion; we die, but we live!

Regardless of whether we've had a good day or a bad one, the resurrection has had an effect on our day. I love the appearance of the risen Christ in John's Gospel:

> On the evening of that first day of the week, when the doors were locked, where the disciples were, for fear of the Jews, Jesus came and stood in their midst and said to them, "Peace be with you." When he had said this, he showed them his hands and his side. The disciples rejoiced when they saw the Lord. [Jesus] said to them again, "Peace be with you. As the Father has sent me, so I send you." And when he had said this, he breathed on them and said to them, "Receive the holy Spirit."
>
> JOHN 20:19-22

The disciples were probably locked away in the room where they had a meal a few nights earlier. They were at a wake of sorts, telling stories, laughing a bit, and crying a lot. Jesus literally breaks in through the locked doors to let them know he is alive. What I find fascinating is this: he doesn't explain death, suffering, eternal life or loss. He wishes them, "Peace." That was enough; our suffering is not in vain!

I think this speaks to our lives as well. The resurrection is the gift of peace to a people plagued with stress and anxiety. Our questions may go unanswered, our suffering unexplained, but the promise is the gift of the Spirit, the gift of peace. These readings are used on Pentecost, the feast of the birthday of our church. It makes sense because that is who we have become as his disciples—people who have seen the risen Lord in the gift of peace.

I also know some people who work hard to keep the doors locked. I call these people the half-empty people. They're the ones who always see the lack—the half-empty glass. Put a lot of them in your life, the locks will be tightly bolted. Seek positive influences in your life and the doors can swing open much more easily.

We need people in our lives who remind us of the resurrection. I vividly remember concelebrating the funeral of the father of a brother and sister in our school. He was also an alumnus of St. John's and was so proud to have his children attending the same school. When he found out he had a brain tumor, Dave decided to live each day to the fullest. His friends gathered at the school before he died and threw a huge party for him. He danced and laughed with his family and friends all night long. At his funeral I witnessed a most profound experience of the resurrection. The celebrant of the Mass knew him since he was a young child, two of his friends spoke lovingly about their friend and his teenage daughter, spoke eloquently of the love her family had for this wonderful man. Afterwards, I shared with his daughter, in words that fell far short of my feelings, that the funeral was tragically sad but totally joyful because they knew the resurrection so well.

People who are gifted in this way are such examples to the rest of us! They call us to more, they challenge us to change our perception of suffering and death. No, Dave is not dead, he lives with Jesus in the resurrection and that is good news to us!

~ 5 ~

The Third Step:
Survey of Actions

The crowds almost crushed him. And a woman afflicted
with hemorrhages for twelve years, who [had spent her
whole livelihood on doctors and] was unable to be cured
by anyone, came up behind him and touched the tassel
on his cloak. Immediately her bleeding stopped. Jesus
then asked, "Who touched me?" While all were denying
it, Peter said, "Master, the crowds are pushing and pressing in upon you." But Jesus said, "Someone has touched
me; for I know that power has gone out from me." When
the woman realized that she had not escaped notice, she
came forward trembling. Falling down before him, she
explained in the presence of all the people why she had
touched him and how she had been healed immediately.
He said to her, "Daughter, your faith has saved you; go
in peace."

LUKE 8:42-48

I LOVE THIS PASSAGE. Think about the scene; there's a
crowd, everyone is pressing against each other to get a
glimpse of or to touch Jesus. In the midst of the commo-

tion, a woman touches him, and he knows it. His friends think he is crazy. It's a mob scene. But, he knew he was touched.

This is the epitome of someone in tune with the step called "survey of actions." Each moment of life is a moment with the potential for the power of God to break in. In some ways this is the easiest of the steps of the Examen, but it takes a lifetime to manage. It's easy to think of God's presence in the special moments of our day: in rising, at prayer, and before bed. It's also easy to think of God in the special moments of life: birth, marriage, and love.

But in the middle of our day, in the routine events of our lives, in the gatherings around the water cooler, on the phone, on the road, or at the supermarket, things become a bit more challenging. Those in-between moments can become mundane and insignificant.

That is why the prayer for enlightenment precedes this moment. An enlightened heart sees more moments of God than an unenlightened one. The problem is this: in the mob scene of our lives, it is easy to miss the individual touch of God. Once we know the touch, there is a necessary response. We cannot go on living as if things are the same. Once we are enlightened, darkness is no longer an option.

We have all been enlightened to an extent, and to an extent, we are all obligated to live as people touched by Jesus, especially during the in-between moments. Of course, the converse of this is true as well. Not only does God use each moment of our day to touch us, God uses us to touch others throughout the day.

I remember a great old story I heard years ago, and it

still rings true today. During World War II some American soldiers were going through a town destroyed by bombs and one of them realized it was Sunday. They looked for a church to say a prayer, but all of the churches had been destroyed. All that was left of the small Catholic church in the town was a brick wall with a statue of the Sacred Heart. The statue had been damaged in the bombing and both arms of Jesus were broken off. The soldiers gathered around the statue and began to pray. One soldier turned away and said, "I cannot pray to this image of Jesus, it is broken and damaged." Another soldier picked up a slab of plaster and etched into it the phrase, "Now you must be my arms." He hung it around the neck of the statue and the soldier said he never forgot how meaningful that moment was. He realized that he too was called to be the arms and hands of Jesus. He was called to be a healer, reconciler, and lover.

As people who survey our actions or reflect on our daily lives, we first must seek how we have been the person of Christ to others. The image of Jesus as healer, reconciler, and lover are good images to reflect upon in order to see Jesus' presence through our lives each day.

Jesus the Healer

It is quite obvious throughout the life of Jesus that he was a healer. People who were in his presence felt touched, felt cared for, felt better just because they were with him. We have a great capacity to act in the name of Jesus as healers. In a sense, it is in this capacity that we have the potential to share in his life and ministry. We have an ability to make others feel cared for that is quite powerful. I can think of countless times that I have been in the back of the church after Mass and someone says, "Father, when you spoke, I felt it was Jesus talking to me through you." I can't even remember having said the words sometimes, but I know in spite of me, Jesus broke through to heal the person.

It may sound a bit simplistic, but we have a real capacity to make a person's day better. A kind word, a sincere thought, a "thank-you" can make their burdens much lighter. Generally, no one can heal a broken heart or broken spirit but the broken person, but as members of Christ's body we certainly can make the burden a bit lighter. I have some friends like that in my own life. People who send me cards to remind me that I am lovable and that I make a difference. That experience has only urged me on to do the same to those around me.

I rarely hear anyone say, "I like recognition." Most people take on the mask of humility. Yet, if we look deep within, we can probably acknowledge that to some extent, it is nice to be noticed for doing what we do well. Knowing that about ourselves, we must assume it is true for others. I liken it to the scene in John's Gospel where Jesus gives his apostles the gift of the Holy Spirit:

> The disciples rejoiced when they saw the Lord. [Jesus] said to them again, "Peace be with you. As the Father has sent me, so I send you." And when he had said this, he breathed on them and said to them, "Receive the holy Spirit. Whose sins you forgive are forgiven them, and whose sins you retain are retained."
>
> JOHN 20:21-23

Jesus tells his disciples quite plainly, you can heal, you can forgive sins, you can make people whole by how you possess this Spirit that I am giving to you. In the name of Jesus, we are able to accomplish great things. The sacrament of reconciliation provides us with the gift of the Spirit as well. The Spirit is the Spirit; no one gets more or less. It's how we possess it, how we use it that makes all the difference. Jesus challenges us to live a life worthy of our call—to reach out concretely to those around us and make lives better by virtue of our gift of the Spirit. It can happen in as many ways as we will allow, as long as we are committed to being the arms and hands of our Lord.

Jesus as Reconciler

When I am invited to speak to a group, I sometimes ask how many people are mad at someone or know someone who is mad at someone. Inevitably almost every hand in the group shoots into the air! Have you ever met someone who found it impossible to say "I'm sorry"? Usually these are the ones who have a long list of people that they are not talking to! Life by it's very nature has bumps and bruises but with the gift of healing comes the gift of reconciling. Admittance of wrongdoing is basically an admittance of our humanity. Good-meaning people can and do hurt one another; good-meaning people can and do say some pretty rotten things!

Sometimes we realize how much we love someone after we hurt them. We get a terrible feeling in the pit of our stomach, and after the hurt has subsided, we feel terrible. I remember hurting one of my closest friends very deeply with my big mouth one time. He left my house outraged, and my stomach began to bother me right away. I couldn't go to sleep that night without apologizing for being such an idiot! Sometimes though, it is much harder to heal broken relationships. It is very hard to heal a relationship which has ended abruptly or ended in death. Through amazing grace, even in these circumstances, there are possibilities for miracles.

I am the chaplain at a Catholic High School. Losing my sister to leukemia during my teenage years, I am very sensitive to students who have suffered losses. One of our kids lost his dad in a tragic accident five years ago. Kevin is still working through all the feelings of grief: anger, disappointment, loneliness, sorrow, guilt, etc. The agreement we have is simple: when he needs to work "stuff" out between him and his dad, he can come to my office and ask me to bring him to the cemetery. He has taken me up on the offer a few times, and I have been moved to quiet tears at the scene. We go after school; he is quiet in the car. When we get to the grave, he gets out and stares for a long while but a great deal is happening on the inside. It is a moment of reconciliation. I say nothing; it is a very humbling experience. I drive him back to school, and after a while, we can talk about the experience. It is amazing to be in the holy presence of their love and watch healing take place. Jesus' words, "Your faith has healed you," ring truer than ever.

Addicted or not, living or deceased, abandoned or abused, to be the arms and hands of the Jesus of love, we have to reconcile our broken relationships.

Jesus of Love

It has almost become a cliché to say "Love one another." It sounds like a sixties leftover. But that is what Jesus did—loved. If we want to get close to God, we have to get close to love. Love does make us vulnerable; love can leave us brokenhearted. I am reminded of the verse in Deuteronomy:

> [Make justice] your aim, that you may have life and may possess the land which the LORD, your God, is giving you.
>
> DEUTERONOMY 16:20

In a world of rampant sexual harassment and abuse charges, and "hands-off" work policies, it can be difficult to love well. I remember when I was a seminarian intern at St. Anthony's in Rocky Point, New York, I was truly loved by the people of God. People would hug, kiss and embrace me after Mass. It was like having hundreds of family members! That expression of love on the part of the parish was enough to convince me that priestly ministry, though difficult and lonely at times, can be a great source of love and affection. Those people called me to priesthood from their love.

To act in the name of Jesus is to do just that—to call others forth through love. We must ask ourselves through this survey of actions, "Did I love well today?"

People may say they don't need anyone, but we all need to love and be loved. Jesus needed to be loved, too. Throughout the Gospels we hear about the disciple's love for Jesus, and how the crowds (not unlike the people in Rocky Point) hemmed in on Jesus to hug him and to love him.

Jesus had to show his love as well. He needed people like Lazarus and John the Disciple, whom scripture tells us he loved. We are called to imitate Jesus the Lover.

I am preparing to celebrate my tenth anniversary in the priesthood. At first glance, I thought a nice dinner out with my family would suffice. As I thought about it, it is a bigger day than my immediate family. Hundreds of people have called me to priesthood day after day for the last ten years. It is not a celebration of me, it is a celebration of them, and of how they were and are the love of Jesus for me. So we are going to have a party, and a great one at that! It will hopefully be a day to celebrate the friendship and community that Jesus uses to call me to his service. A true celebration of Jesus' love for his people!

Some years ago I read a book that literally changed my life. *Urgent Longings* by Thomas Tyrrel is basically a book about how hard it is for human beings to love well and be successful in relationships. The book's title comes from the beginning of John of the Cross' poem, *The Dark Night of the Soul:*

One dark night,
fired with love's urgent longings
—Ah, the sheer grace!—
I went out unseen,
My house being no wall stilled.

It didn't take me long to notice that in my life "urgent longings" play a major role. Urgent longings occur when we try to love too hard, we try to possess, to own, or to control. Loving well is work! It takes a balance of free-dom and trust to really love someone and let them be free. Think of marriage. Couples get married, but they cannot possibly spend every waking minute with each other. They work, they see their "own" friends, they need time alone.

The point is that no relationship can be successful unless those qualities of freedom and trust are present. We will be unsuccessful with our children, with our spouses, with our friends, and with anyone we love unless we encounter love's urgent longings head-on.

Most of the problems in relationships involve infatua-tion. We think we are loving, but we are not. We are lust-ing, controlling, or fearful, but we are not loving. Love frees us and love frees those we love! Part of our survey of actions has to be an honest look at our love relation-ships. We must ask ourselves some tough questions. Am I infatuated or am I in love? Why don't I feel lovable? Why can't I let the ones I love be who they are?

I admit it takes a great deal of "soul work," but to truly survey our actions we must look to our motiva-tions. I work in a high school and I see many young peo-ple infatuated with each other. They are so vulnerable at this stage. He says something and she is crying. She says something and he is not talking to her. I spend hours in my office each week with young people in this state. They are a mess! Mondays are always the worst. Over the weekend is when everything happens; the "he said, she said," the time spent with "other friends," or the now classic, "he/she didn't call me."

I am not making light of these adolescent problems. They are real and they hurt. I have come to see over the years that they are not just adolescent problems. Many of us have grown to adulthood with an adolescent approach to relationships. It makes for inordinate stress and anxiety in relationships.

How do we triumph over this? I have bad news. We can't. We have to live through it: the pain, the rejection, the suffering, until we can grow through infatuation to a deeper love. Surveying our actions can help us to tag these emotions and to name them as part of our spiritual journey. That doesn't take away the pain of urgent longings, but it certainly can help them to challenge us to grow.

I used to pray each day for people to truly love in my life. Now I pray to love the people in my life truly! My plate is full and I still have a lot of work to do!

If I could rub a lamp and make a wish I really think I would wish to love the people in my life well. I wish it was as easy as a blink of the eye. But it takes time. It's a process. That's why it so important to survey our actions, so that we can see the progress. It keeps us honest. It's like going to Weight Watchers. You can say all you like about losing weight, but the scale keeps you honest!

Perhaps losing weight has a lot in common with loving well. Weight loss is slow and a bit painstaking. Love happens the same way; it develops, you become. St. Ignatius made provision for this in his Spiritual Exercises. He refers to this process as "the conversion of the small part of the heart." Conversion, love, faith, and the like happen a bit at a time. It's a process.

I keep a piece of the Berlin Wall on my desk as a reminder of this. I always think of how the wall came down. Students bore holes in the wall and for the first time could look at each other. Then they made the holes larger so they could shake hands through the wall. At last they broke through, one piece at a time, until the wall was gone. I like having the concrete rock on my desk because I constantly need to be reminded of what it represents: freedom is a process, one piece at a time. It's so important to know this; personal happiness hinges on it. The other thing that the rock reminds me of is that we need to celebrate the small victories, the small conversions of the heart.

In a way, St. Paul gives conversion a bad name! At a quick glance, it seems that he just got thrown on the ground and immediately changed his life. The process of the event is lost:

On that journey as I drew near to Damascus, about noon a great light from the sky suddenly shone around me. I fell to the ground and heard a voice saying to me, "Saul, Saul, why are you persecuting me?" I replied, "Who are you, sir?" And he said to me, "I am Jesus the Nazorean whom you are persecuting. My companions saw the light but did not hear the voice of the one who spoke to me." I asked, "What shall I do, sir?" The Lord answered me, "Get up and go into Damascus, and there you will be told about everything appointed for you to do." Since I could see nothing because of the brightness of that light, I was led by hand by my companions and entered Damascus.

A certain Ananias, a devout observer of the law, and highly spoken of by all the Jews who lived there, came to me and stood there and said, "Saul, my brother, regain your sight." And at that very moment I regained my sight and saw him. Then he said, "The God of our ancestors designated you to know his will, to see the Righteous One, and to hear the sound of his voice; for you will be his witness before all to what you have seen and heard.

Now, why delay? Get up and have yourself baptized and your sins washed away, calling upon his name."

ACTS 22:6-16

It seems too neat and pre-packaged at a quick glance. It encourages us to think the same way of conversion in our own lives. Let me see the light and that will solve all my problems! Yet, in reality this was a lifelong process for Paul. It involved a lot of soul searching, tears, and struggle. That's the good part of the news! We are not alone in our heartaches and pain. The victories will be small, but they will add up. They will lead to conversion. We need to add up these victories. That's where the survey of actions plays an integral role.

I am always put off by the claim of "self-made millionaires." Who is self-made? The psalmist reminds us in Psalm 139: "You search me and you know me, you knit me together in my mother's womb." Through the amazing gift of grace we have become who we are. This doesn't happen in a vacuum, it happens in the midst of family, friends, and community. That's what love is all about, and Jesus epitomizes the gift of this love.

~ 6 ~

The Fourth Step:
Contrition and Sorrow

I SPEND A PART OF MY LIFE as a priest hearing confessions. In many ways it is the most draining "work" that I do as a priest. I love crowds, they energize me. One-on-one in the powerful sacrament of reconciliation, I am quickly exhausted. Over the years, I have come to appreciate the first confession services that I participate in. In many ways these are moments that the whole family can use to reflect and renew their involvement in the life of our church. Some time ago I was celebrating the sacrament with second graders. They were taught the Act of Contrition, and told to make up their own prayer to Jesus. One little girl began her prayer, "Oh my God I am *partly* sorry for having offended you." I chuckled to myself and began correcting the little girl by saying you must mean *heartily* sorry not partly sorry. She quickly responded, "No Father, I mean *partly* because part of it was his fault!"

What is contrition all about? What is a contrite spirit? For me it is summed up in the word "regret." Did you ever do something and regret it immediately, but it was too late? This important fourth step of the Consciousness Examen calls us to visit the regrets of our lives, the regrets of our days together. At the outset it is important to say that we do not dwell here. The Examen specifically says visit this moment of our lives. It is not a time for self-hate or unhealthy guilt. Look at the regrets, acknowledge them and then enter the second moment; be sorry.

In one of his songs Elton John sings, "Sorry seems to be the hardest word." For many of us admitting fault is a very difficult moment. Yet Jesus teaches that it is integral to health and life with him. Acknowledge your sins and know God's forgiveness. Think about the woman caught in adultery:

> They said to him, "Teacher, this woman was caught in the very act of committing adultery. Now in the law, Moses commanded us to stone such women. So what do you say?" They said this to test him, so that they could have some charge to bring against him. Jesus bent down and began to write on the ground with his finger.
>
> But when they continued asking him, he straightened up and said to them, "Let the one among you who is without sin be the first to throw a stone at her." Again he bent down and wrote on the ground. And in response, they went away one by one, beginning with the elders. So he was left alone with the woman before him. Then Jesus straightened up and said to her, "Woman, where are they? Has no one condemned you?" She replied, "No one, sir." Then Jesus said, "Neither do I condemn you. Go, [and] from now on avoid this sin."
>
> JOHN 8:4-11

Jesus helped the would-be stone throwers to examine their consciences and they left regretting what had happened that day. At the same time, Jesus accepted the woman's regret and literally transformed it to something completely freeing. She left that scene a different woman, a changed person. It would be impossible for her to live the same way again, because she knew she had been touched deeply through her own act of contrition and sorrow. The same thing happens to us when we are touched by Jesus' healing love; we are changed; we are not the same any more. The crosses, the mistakes are often the first doorway to salvation for us.

All my life I have had a struggle with weight. It boils down to something far less psychological than some would say. I love to eat! I love to celebrate life at the table with people I love. I truly dislike eating alone. I love a great meal with friends. As you can imagine, I have been on every diet imaginable. Some time ago I went on an all-liquid diet that was coupled with psychological counseling and medical care. The counseling group I was in was quite funny. There were twelve members, with only two men in the group. The other man was the owner of a series of very famous and prestigious steak houses throughout the country. While everyone else was talking about how much they hated themselves, and how they would sneak food at various times of the day, we were comparing notes on who made the best steak sauce, and served the best steaks.

During a break in our session, he pulled me aside and promised that when we finished this diet, he would treat me to the best steak of my life at his place! I lived for that night! We spoke to each other like inmates waiting for parole.

I knew great success on that diet, though it was passing! In the end I lost 122 pounds. I was skinny, I was a bit pale and yes, I had a wonderful steak dinner during my "parole." But I wasn't going to be skinny for long. My first night on solid food in six months was spent at a Met game at Shea Stadium. I remember seeing the hot dog lady come around. I was with all my friends; I felt free for the first time in months. All I remember was taking $20 out of my wallet and ordering three hot dogs! It was as if I was skinny for a day.

I remember asking the psychologist, who also had a belly, what was wrong with me. He said, "Nothing is wrong with you, you are human, and you have to be who you are." In some ways he gave me permission to let go of the terrible regret I had in letting myself get fat again. I felt freed. Now don't get me wrong, I advocate a healthy lifestyle, and I still struggle everyday, but to live in fear, regret and sorrow leaves us much less human than we could be.

For most of us, the same sins follow us around all of our lives. We're not adulterers one minute and embezzlers the next. No, the cross doesn't change that much. It is the same character faults, prejudices and weaknesses that burden us all of our lives. There are times that we do pretty well, but there are undeniably times when we fail miserably. The spiritual moment occurs when we do something with the failures. This step in the Consciousness Examen calls us to reflect with regret on the failure, but more importantly to let it go. As Jesus tells the woman, "Go and try to avoid this sin in the future." The line almost implies future failings! Jesus knew that it would be a struggle for this woman, but she was forgiven anyway. Jesus re-establishes her self love and gives her the strength for a series of small victories that lead her back to wholeness.

In any life it seems that it is the small victories that help us carry the crosses better. That is why we need to reflect daily on our sins. Contrition and sorrow help us to know we are human. They help us to acknowledge that we need help and that we need healing. I am not advocating daily confession. I am advocating not kidding ourselves.

There are times in the sacrament of reconciliation where someone will come in and say, "It has been three years since my last confession, and in that time I haven't committed any sins." What? I think to myself. They should go out to the statue of Mary, push it off the pedestal and climb up there! To be in touch spiritually is to know our sins. They really are nothing to be ashamed of, they make us human. They are the marks of humanity.

I am always taken by the resurrection account in John's Gospel (20:19-20):

> On the evening of that first day of the week, when the doors were locked, where the disciples were, for fear of the Jews, Jesus came and stood in their midst and said to them, "Peace be with you." When he had said this, he showed them his hands and his side. The disciples rejoiced when they saw the Lord.

The risen Jesus still had wounds. I have thought about that for a long time. Why would God leave the wounds on his son after the resurrection. I think it connects very deeply with the idea that our wounds, our sins, are the way we get in contact with the risen Jesus. Our wounds lead us to Him! They are the pathway to the resurrection. Jesus' wounds are really our sins, and now they have been transformed. To be human is not to be perfect. It is to acknowledge the wounds we inflict and the wounds that have been inflicted upon us. I always say that "nothing is for nothing." In the scriptures, everything has a reason and a purpose. In this case, the wounds of Jesus offer us hope. The struggles of our lives can be transformed to something holy, to a way to God. There indeed is hope for the overeaters among us and for the adulterers and embezzlers, too!

For The Sins of My Past Life

It is relatively easy to accept God's forgiveness for our sinfulness. As we reflect each day on how we hurt others, or hurt ourselves, it is a wonderful reality that we are forgiven. The difficulty comes in forgiving ourselves. I ask myself where the statement "for the sins of my past life" came from. Do we have prior lives? Do we need to ask for forgiveness again for sins we asked forgiveness for in the past or is there something deeper going on here. Could we be seeking forgiveness for the sins that we have not yet forgiven ourselves for?

In some ways, God's forgiveness is a bit too easy. It involves no real trial, it just involves seeking forgiveness, and it is given freely. *Seems too easy; there's got to be a catch somewhere.* Yet, there is no catch unless we refuse to forgive ourselves. With God there is no past life, but

with us there is and so we make forgiveness more difficult by beating ourselves up and putting ourselves
down. How does this happen?

I think it has to do with original sin. However won-
derfully we are made, being human involves being
vulnerable. When we are vulnerable we have doubts,
especially in regard to loving and being loved. The
doubts lead to a lack of self respect, and even to self hate.

I don't mean to sum up original sin in one paragraph.
But if you think back to any sin that you repeatedly commit, it usually stems from a lack of self love. The woman
caught in the act of adultery probably did not understand that she was a child of God or respect herself very
much. She probably doubted her lovability and saw this
as the only way to know love. She didn't know the difference between love with a small "l" and love with a
capital "L."

"L"ove versus "l"ove

I always explain Love, love that touches the divine, as
the love we have for a spouse or a very dear friend or
family member. These are the people we see the most
and often when we are at our worst. If we treated our
business associates the way we treat those we "love,"
we'd have no friends left! Why do "we always hurt the
ones we love. . ." and why do they love us anyway?

I think it is because they see the core of who we are—
that ultimately we are lovable and good people. They
see what we often do not see in ourselves and that we
must love ourselves before we can love others. How
often we've heard Jesus' great commandment: "Love

one another as yourself" and how often we forget the "as yourself" part! So how can we begin to love ourselves better?

It begins with this step in the Examen—letting go of our brokenness, and recognizing that we must move on. In fact we are compelled to move on. It's kind of sad to see people who live in the past. For whatever reason, their identity was lost in a moment and they never left that moment. They love who they were, not who they are. It can happen to anyone—we can get stuck in our high school days, when we were the stars on the field or when we could dance without losing our breath! In that moment we may even say we loved ourselves, but it was fleeting. Look in the mirror now—at who you are today. The true spiritual moment is when we can look at the old pictures and say, it was fun, but now it's even better!

As I mentioned, I am celebrating ten years as a priest. It has caused me to look back at some pictures of my first blessings, and my first Mass. I look at those pictures and start to laugh because I have changed so much in ten years! Thank God for that! I have shown some of these pictures to friends and they say things like, "Wow, you got older," "You lost a lot of hair since then," and "Is that really you?" I must admit as I look at some of the pictures, I too am shocked that I once looked so innocent and young. Although I am in good health, I look older; even a bit beat up as I prepare to turn forty!

In all honesty I wouldn't choose to go back. Things have gotten better and better, my sense of purpose and meaning has only grown over the past ten years as has my relationship with Jesus. So I look a little beat up. So what! The point of being human is to empty ourselves, use ourselves up in the service of the Lord. I really believe that. Look in the mirror today, look at an old picture, too. Are you happy where you are? What could make you happier? Can you love yourself better?

This is the struggle of being human—to love ourselves in the present tense. We cannot really use the Consciousness Examen to its fullest potential unless we can truly love ourselves with our brokenness. The step of contrition and sorrow gives us a way to do this by enabling forgiveness every moment of our lives which helps us to encounter the brokenness head on and to move on.

Embracing Brokenness

If I ever write another book (which I sincerely doubt!), I would love to title it "Embracing Brokenness." I really think that it is necessary to acknowledge the brokenness of our lives in order to live the holiness of our lives.

When are we whole (holy)? If your life is like mine, we don't feel whole too often. We may get glimpses of who we could be, but for the most part, we feel like damaged goods. I used to feel terrible about myself for this. Then I read a book by the great author Henri Nouwen titled *The Wounded Healer.* Nouwen states that we are called to heal one another but must realize that we are wounded as well. We go through life with the cracks in our lives, but they can be filled with the love of God. It leaves us wounded, but repaired!

My Aunt Mary had a beautiful "high Italian" living room. It was covered in plastic, meticulously dusted and kept. She had many things on display: holy pictures, plates, ceramics, things her grandchildren made, and a

Venetian ceramic angel that was hauling in a net full of fish. Why do I remember that statue? Because I broke it. Like many Italian homes, when family came over, the adults went to the basement, and the children were relegated to another room to watch television and have their own party.

I remember throwing a pillow at my cousin Philip and knocking the statue off the pedestal onto the floor, where it broke into a million little pieces. We spent the rest of the day working diligently at gluing the statue together. We were like Italian artisans rushing to finish a piece of art for the dedication of a basilica in Rome! When we were finished, the statue looked like it had been dipped in glue. It was very obvious that it was smashed. Her hand was missing, the fishing net was put together wrong, little pieces were still on the floor. But we placed the statue back on the pedestal and hoped for the best.

At the end of the night, everyone came upstairs and said good night. I knew that Aunt Mary saw the broken statue. I saw her look at it, look at us and go on talking. She never said a word to anyone, as far as I know. In addition, she kept that broken statue on that pedestal for years and years. I would go visit her as an adult and laugh to myself looking at the statue. There was no way she didn't know. She dusted everything every day. But maybe the statue became more valuable to her after it was broken. It was more than just a statue then. It was a statue with a tremendous act of love (and fear!) attached to it. It may have reminded her of the playfulness of youth, the celebration of family, or the fragility of relationships.

As much as we may try to avoid it, things are going to get broken. Just like Humpty Dumpty, all the pieces don't go back together again perfectly. It's true in everybody's lives. Maybe we need a broken statue around to remind us of our brokenness and our beauty. A creative person doesn't throw something away when it is broken; they find a new use for it.

We need to recognize that we have fallen off the pedestal a few times. We are chipped and broken, but not garbage. We are wounded healers called to love others as we love ourselves— wounds and all!

I also think that television and the media have a great deal to do with our dislike of ourselves or our embarrassment with who we are. I grew up watching *The Brady Bunch* and *The Partridge Family.* They were great shows, and established quite a cult following, even to this day. There was one huge problem: there was never a problem on either show that couldn't be solved in a half hour with some laughs and maybe even a song.

For my money, that's just not life! But as a kid, I thought it was. In looking at my own life and the life of my family, we had problems. My sister was dying, my family was in turmoil, I lost myself in her sickness, and we couldn't solve the problem in a half hour; no laugh tracks either, and very little music.

Looking back, those shows did a certain disservice to our generation. As a matter of fact, they worked hard to preserve the false image of family harmony. Now we know the stories of struggle behind the scenes of these shows: stories of drug and alcohol abuse, inappropriate sexual expression, depression, bitter grudges, and lack of compassion. Some of these may sound more like home for us! Actually, I remember on *The Partridge Family*, one of the children, the actor who played the drums, was replaced. I read later that the first actor was a problem because his parents interfered with the production, so he was fired. Ever wish you could do that in your family? Hire a new son or daughter to take the role over?

Fortunately, that is not reality. Our family brokenness can't be renegotiated, we can't fire and hire family. But we can help ourselves to accept and love the family we have been given by God. I find that with family, comparisons always fall short. When we are compared to other parents, when we compare our kids to other kids, or siblings to other siblings, we set ourselves up for trouble. Hating ourselves and where we have come from will leave us isolated and alone.

Integration of our families, ourselves, and our life situations are paramount to emotional and spiritual health. We need to pray earnestly to let go of past pain and hurt inflicted upon us by ourselves or by others.

I know a family that has a son who was addicted to drugs and alcohol. After much prayer and reflection they locked him out of the house. He lived on the street for six weeks until he finally agreed to get help for his addiction. At this time, the family has integrated all their pain and frustration and their son is a healthy, active member of the family again. Miracles can happen, if we allow them to. There is a certain openness to the spirit and a willingness to do the work, that allows us to be forgiven and healed.

It's much the same as Alcoholics Anonymous. God does the work, but unless we are open to God's healing, it cannot happen. There has to be a higher power. If we try to be God, we end up frustrated time and time again. Why? Well, the answer is simple, only God is God. We must be who we are now and willing to become more each day.

To become what we receive—the body of Christ—we must be people who love ourselves. That fills us with peace and joy because we experience the miracle of healing that God offers. Buy a bouquet of flowers for yourself; treat yourself to a slice of pizza or a nice ice cream cone. You're worth it. Then, love your neighbor as yourself.

~ 7 ~

The Fifth Step:
Resolution for Future

THE WORD *RESOLUTION* gets a bad reputation because of New Year's Eve, but the definition of the word speaks of perseverance and steadfastness. Not an unrealistic goal, but a vow to abide, and to continue to work at all our lives.

This final step of the Examen calls us to persevere in our commitment to the future. It calls us to be future-oriented people, to be new. For some of us, this will be the most difficult part of the Examen. It calls us to commit to growth, to welcome change, to remain steadfast regardless of what happens. It is truly difficult to be a person of resolution.

A big joke among my close friends is related to this. Whenever I begin something new in my life, whether it be a retreat, a diet, a new assignment, a friendship, a new "whatever," I respond that I am a "new man." My friends tell me that they have never met anyone who has been made a new man so many times!

Although we laugh at this together, I guess it is because I really believe on some level that we do become "new" after meaningful experiences in our lives. I remember when I went on a thirty-day silent retreat. It was a life-changing experience. I came home proclaiming myself a new man. I remember going to Dachau, the concentration camp, and coming home a new man. I remember a trip to Medjugorge, and the same occurred. Maybe I was never totally new after these experiences, but something certainly happened.

What was it; what is it that changes us as we move to the future? I think love is at the heart of it all. To know love is to be changed. I recently visited friends of mine who just had their first child. The night before the birth, Jen and Victor said, "we can't wait until tomorrow, our lives will be changed forever with the birth of our son!" I went to the hospital the next day and visited them and their four-hour old child. Tears of joy just came to my eyes when I saw Jen with little Ryan in her arms. She was a new woman, never to be the same again after knowing such love.

Every day invites us to newness, new possibilities, new hopes, and new dreams. How does one become a person of "resolution for the future?" In some ways it is the life journey, in other ways it is a simple *fiat*, like the Blessed Mother's "yes." Either way it takes faith and commitment to pray this last step well.

There are definite characteristics of a person resolved for the future. They are the great hope for our church; the visioners of a new millennium. I would like to touch upon five characteristics of people resolved for the future using five people from the scriptures: Mary, John the Baptist, Paul, Joseph of Arimathea, and Martha.

Mary: Your will be done

Mary said, "Behold, I am the handmaid of the Lord. May it be done to me according to your word." Then the angel departed from her.

LUKE 1:38

What a great thing to be able to do! Mary could trust so much in the presence of God that she could say, *your will be done.* To be a future-oriented person, we must be able to say these words, too. Our prayer must be that nothing will happen that we cannot get through with the help of God.

I tend to be a *"your will with a little help from my will"* person. I have a hard time surrendering to God, I'll admit it! As I get older, I see the value in letting someone else drive the bus. It just makes more sense. As a young man, I was in a seminary system that prepared you for a specific goal: priesthood. Why did we study, why pray, why do anything? The goal was always there. For some, after the goal was met, there was a real sense of "now what?" It was difficult to find direction when so much of our lives was oriented toward one goal.

This is not unlike a couple getting married who plans their wedding for a year. The day comes and goes, and then it is time to start living. But, they don't know how to live, because their future was oriented toward one day and one specific moment.

Mary had the ability to walk with God in such a powerful way that she could be totally free in letting go of her control and opening herself to being a servant of

God. We need that too! Can we say yes to a walk with cancer, a divorce, a gay son or daughter, a job loss, or a death in our family? Your will be done. It doesn't seem fair; it doesn't seem right; but your will be done. The Blessed Mother gives us wonderful food for thought; to become his body, we need to let go.

John the Baptist: Prepare the way of the Lord

A man named John was sent from God. He came for testimony, to testify to the light, so that all might believe through him. He was not the light, but came to testify to the light.

JOHN 1:6-8

A true man of the future! It was John's job to get people ready. Perhaps John was the consummate man of the last step of the Examen. His life pointed beyond himself to others. He knew that there was something more to come and that he would be privileged enough to see it to fruition. John lived in the *hope that there was more to come!*

Do we possess that same vision? Are we able to point beyond ourselves to that which is to come? In reality, we may have to admit we like our world to revolve around ourselves. We don't like waiting. We're a fast food generation. The same can be true in spirituality. We may want to have a relationship with Jesus now without the work, without the waiting.

I don't like to place orders through catalogs—too much waiting, can't really know what you're getting. But some of life is just like that—not knowing what's coming. There is a degree of anticipating or waiting but it can be adventurous if we let it!

Christmas shopping at the mall is a wonderful example of my disdain for waiting. I do everything possible to avoid the reality of going, but when I must, I bring a book, a walkman, a cellular phone, a snack, and a pen to entertain me. God forbid I should have twenty minutes alone with myself! In my experience no one likes to wait. Yet, John the Baptist was a great *waiter.*

He knew that his world did not revolve around himself. He knew that patience would give way to excitement about the presence of God-made-human. He didn't mind waiting! A great part of preparation is waiting. Can we commit to waiting well, to pointing beyond our own lives—beyond our busy agendas—and point to *someone else*, to *something else* that may need our attention in the days to come? I pray a lot to be more like John; a bit radical, but one who prepares the way, moves others along and excites the crowd to anticipate the in-breaking of God.

Paul: We are the body of Christ

Now you are Christ's body, and individually parts of it.
1 CORINTHIANS 12:27

Not unlike most Catholics, I love Paul! He is so passionate, so direct, and yet so spiritual. I mentioned earlier that I end each homily I give with the words, "Pray that we may more fully become what we receive from that altar today, the Body of Christ." That is a prayer of resolution for future. *Help me to be His body today;* let me be his loving hands and heart.

Joseph of Arimathea: A good and upright man

> Having bought a linen cloth, he took him down, wrapped him in the linen cloth and laid him in a tomb that had been hewn out of the rock. Then he rolled a stone against the entrance to the tomb.
>
> MARK 15:46

Joseph of Arimathea is a very interesting figure; he is the follower of Jesus who prepared him for the resurrection. He was a man of vision, and when you think about it, he was quite fearless. He could have been killed as a sympathizer for coming forward and asking for the body. But he proceeded anyway. *He trusted in the future.* So great was his trust that it was from his tomb, from his linen cloth, and from his love and hope that the resurrection occurs. People who trust in the future are encouraging people. They help others to see that there is more.

In my family, there was such a man. Al and his family own a pizzeria in the Hamptons, on Long Island. He was a joyful person, loved life, his family and friends. On another level, he was a quiet disciple of Jesus. Al never received an award for a heroic life, or recognition for his contribution to the church, but in his own way, he was a person of hope, who called others to trust in the future. How? He did it over slices of pizza, over the phone, however God asked him. Owning a pizzeria is sort of like owning a bar. People come in with stories and need to share. Al was a listening ear, in addition to being a source of referral and financial support for many people.

Even when he was diagnosed with cancer, he continued to live as a person of hope. I remember visiting him in the hospital, just days before he died. He assured me that he knew he was going to a place where he would be happy, but more so, he was going to a place where he could continue to help others, and pray for us. That is a person resolved for the future; in the great spirit of Joseph of Arimathea.

My family is not unique in that regard. There are holy people who live with a certain vision of the future. They prepare us for the resurrection by their example. Celebrate these people and pray that we may be people who trust in our own futures through the help of God.

Martha: Anxious about many things

> Now Jesus loved Martha and her sister and Lazarus.
>
> JOHN 11:5

Martha is a great future person! She was always busy *doing*. Her sister Mary couldn't see the value in preparing for the future. She suggested that Martha should just sit and "be" with Jesus. But Martha saw that there was much to do; she was anxious. In every age the church, *the Body of Christ needs people willing to be anxious about the future!* Do you ever worry about the future? Where will I work? How will our kids grow up? What is in store for me? If these questions are familiar, our resolution for the future will be like Martha's. There is much to do, help me Lord to do it well.

We all remember Jesus telling Martha, "Mary has chosen the better part." At that moment, in that setting, perhaps that was true. But without Marthas there is no future! Think about it: there is no celebration of Holy

Week without the anxious planning of many people in the parish; there is no Christmas dinner with our families unless someone plans it, prepares it and serves it; there is no wedding reception without someone attending to all the details.

What I find encouraging is the line, "Jesus loved Martha, and her sister, and Lazarus very much." Jesus loves the future-oriented people as much as the others. No judgment here. He knew that these people were as integral to the life of faith as the others.

Our personality type is not important in light of our resolution for the future. All of us need to make this the last prayer of our Examen. Why? Because the future is coming, regardless of our personality type or whether we are planning well for our futures!

The *resolution for future* is as important as the other four steps of the Consciousness Examen. This final prayer helps us to move through the day filled with hope and the belief that nothing will happen this day that God will not be there with us. For me, this is good news, because every day is like a visit to Disneyworld: Adventureland, Frontierland, Tomorrowland, the Magic Kingdom, and a little Space Mountain too!

~ 8 ~

Conclusion

WE HAVE TRAVELED A JOURNEY together. In some ways, it is a short one, in others it could take a lifetime to complete. I am not a big fan of the self-help market. These books, tapes, videos, calendars tell us how to be effective, how to be happy, skinny, live longer, and in a condescending way, tell us that we don't know what we're doing!

I hope that is not the impression here. First, I barely know what I am doing! Second, this book is in its best sense a *spice*. Anyone who cooks knows that a spice is an important part of any dish. Use too much, it could wreck the meal, use too little, and it has little or no effect. Some people like garlic, everything they make has garlic in it; others like it now and then.

This form of prayer is not meant to be exclusive. It should add to the other parts of our spiritual lives. For me, it is the foundation upon which the rest of my spiritual life is built. I know that God is with me every moment of my day, and so I treat the day, and its occupants accordingly. It doesn't take long to do. Some people spend as little as ten minutes on it, and for others, the rhythm goes on throughout the day in a timeless fashion. It can be prayed at the beginning of a day, the end of a day, four times a day, once a day, however you would like to use the spice!

The bottom line is that the Consciousness Examen has brought me closer to the Creator. After awhile, I wanted to share it with other people. I hope you will grow to share it with those around you.

I mentioned more than once that I end each homily with the line "become what you receive, the body of Christ." On occasion people ask why I always use that line. Is it just an easy way to end a homily? Well, yes, but that is not the reason. It is the line I most remember from the ordination ritual. The bishop reads an instruction from the ritual to the persons to be ordained. In it is the line "become what you receive." It has stuck with me everyday of my life since. It seems to be the goal of the life of a Christian: surrender to me; become my disciple; let me fill you that you may be my heart to the world.

The Consciousness Examen helps that process of becoming. When we see God's intense presence in our lives, we are more fully a disciple and we are more joyful. So let us pray that we recognize God in our lives. Pray that we recognize God's intense presence, so that the world may be one and that we may each day grow closer to becoming what we receive from the table of the Lord, the Body of Christ. Amen.

For Further Reading

Bergan, Jacqueline and Marie Schwan. *Praying with Ignatius of Loyola*. Minnesota: St. Mary's Press, 1991.

Brodrick, James. *Saint Ignatius Loyola: The Pilgrim Years, 1491-1538*. New York: Farrar, Straus and Cudahy, 1956.

Dalmases, Cándido de. *Ignatius of Loyola, Founder of the Jesuits: His Life and Work*. Trans. Jerome Aixalá. Saint Louis: The Institute of Jesuit Sources, 1985.

Fleming, David L. *The Spiritual Exercises of Saint Ignatius: A Literal Translation and a Contemporary Reading*. Saint Louis: The Institute of Jesuit Sources, 1978.

Olin, John C., ed., and Joseph F. O'Callaghan, trans. *The Autobiography of Saint Ignatius Loyola*. New York: Harper and Row, 1974.

Purcell, Mary. *The First Jesuit: Saint Ignatius Loyola (1491-1556)*. Chicago: Loyola University Press, 1981.

Rahner, Karl. *Ignatius of Loyola*. Trans. Rosaleen Oekenden. London: Collins, 1978.

Tetlow, Elisabeth Meier, trans. *The Spiritual Exercises of Saint Ignatius Loyola*. Lanham, MD: University Press of America, 1987.

Young, William J., ed. and trans. *Letters of Saint Ignatius of Loyola*. Chicago: Loyola University Press, 1959.

——, trans. *The Spiritual Journal of Saint Ignatius Loyola, February 1544-1545*. Woodstock, MD: Woodstock College Press, 1958.

Published by Resurrection Press

A Rachel Rosary *Larry Kupferman*	$4.50
Catholic Is Wonderful *Mitch Finley*	$4.95
Christian Marriage *John & Therese Boucher*	$4.95
Come, Celebrate Jesus! *Francis X. Gaeta*	$4.95
From Holy Hour to Happy Hour *Francis X. Gaeta*	$7.95
Glory to Glory *Francis Clare, SSND*	$10.95
The Healing Rosary *Mike D.*	$5.95
Healing through the Mass *Robert DeGrandis, SSJ*	$8.95
Healing the Wounds of Emotional Abuse *Nancy Benvenga*	$6.95
Healing Your Grief *Ruthann Williams, OP*	$7.95
Living Each Day by the Power of Faith *Barbara Ryan*	$8.95
The Joy of Being a Catechist *Gloria Durka*	$4.95
The Joy of Being a Eucharistic Minister *Mitch Finley*	$5.95
Mustard Seeds *Matthew Kelly*	$7.95
Transformed by Love *Margaret Magdalen, CSMV*	$5.95
RVC Liturgical Series: The Liturgy of the Hours	$3.95
The Lector's Ministry	$3.95
Behold the Man *Judy Marley, SFO*	$4.50
Lights in the Darkness *Ave Clark, O.P.*	$8.95
Loving Yourself for God's Sake *Adolfo Quezada*	$5.95
Practicing the Prayer of Presence *van Kaam/Muto*	$7.95
5-Minute Miracles *Linda Schubert*	$4.95
Healthy and Holy under Stress *van Kaam/Muto*	$3.95
Season of New Beginnings *Mitch Finley*	$4.95
Season of Promises *Mitch Finley*	$4.95
Soup Pot *Ethel Pochocki*	$8.95
Stay with Us *John Mullin, SJ*	$3.95
Surprising Mary *Mitch Finley*	$7.95
What He Did for Love *Francis X. Gaeta*	$5.95
You Are My Beloved *Mitch Finley*	$10.95
Your Sacred Story *Robert E. Lauder*	$6.95

For a free catalog call 1-800-892-6657